2009 ROMAN REPLIES & CLSA ADVISORY OPINIONS

25th Anniversary Edition

SR. SHARON A. EUART, R.S.M., J.C.D.
EDITOR, ROMAN REPLIES

MS. SIOBHAN M. VERBEEK, J.C.L.
EDITOR, ADVISORY OPINIONS

CANON LAW SOCIETY OF AMERICA

ISBN 1-932208-24-0
ISSN 1543-4230
SAN 237-6296

Table of Contents

Roman Replies 2009

ADVISORY OPINIONS 2009

FOREWORD

The Canon Law Society of America publishes annually *Roman Replies and CLSA Advisory Opinions* for canonists and those seeking a clearer understanding of the *praxis legis* of the Catholic Church. With the 2009 edition the CLSA commemorates the 25th anniversary of this publication. The combination of these two services, begun in 1984, continues to serve as useful resources for those involved in the application of canonical discipline.

The compilation of materials for *Roman Replies 2009* was guided by Sister Sharon A. Euart, RSM, Executive Coordinator. The collection of entries in this issue, when viewed in conjunction with previous volumes, assists the reader both in understanding recent developments in the law and in identifying current trends in the *praxis* of the Roman Curia.

The selection and assembly of opinions for *CLSA Advisory Opinions 2009* was provided by Ms. Siobhan M. Verbeek, editor. The topics addressed in the opinions reflect a variety of canonical issues and demonstrate the scope of canonical expertise and reflection by members of the Society.

Technical support and cover production for publication of *Roman Replies and CLSA Advisory Opinions 2009* was provided by Katie Richards, Office of the Executive Coordinator.

The *Roman Replies* are collated into successive volumes of the *Canon Law Digest* and periodically *Advisory Opinions* are also collected into larger multi-year volumes, both of which publications are available from the CLSA publications service.

The Canon Law Society of America provides this series as a professional resource. Care should be taken in considering the relative weight of the materials found in this publication. The principles for canonical interpretation (CIC cc. 16-19 and CCEO cc. 1498-1501) serve as guides in considering the contents of this volume.

Sister Sharon A. Euart, RSM
Office of the Executive Coordinator
3025 Fourth Street, NE
The Hecker Center, Suite 111
Washington, DC 20017-1102

Roman Replies

Introductory Note

The following is the editorial policy of Roman Replies. *This policy, as well as the source of these materials, was first described in the 1984 edition and, with some modifications, has been in effect since then.*

Each year all members of the Canon Law Society of America are asked to be on the lookout for, and to submit any recent replies from the various Roman dicasteries which might be of interest to the Society's members and the wider church. Judicial vicars, chancellors, vicars general, major superiors of institutes of consecrated life and societies of apostolic life in the United States, and professors of canon law are encouraged and asked to submit material for this important publication.

To encourage a broad participation in this annual project, all CLSA members are asked to be alert for such materials which may come to their attention.

Finally, contributions from members of the Society resident in other countries or members of other canonical societies are always most welcome. All contributors to *Roman Replies* receive a complimentary copy of the current volume.

Certain editorial principles determine the selection of documents for this publication. First, in general, entries which have already appeared in various canonical journals would not normally be repeated here. An exception is the publication of an official English translation of documents which already has been published in an unofficial translation. Second, documents which merely restate something published earlier with no added nuances or changes are not normally reported. Third, documents that concern a matter not yet resolved by the Roman dicasteries are held for future publication in the hope that the entire matter may be fully reported when the question or controversy has been resolved. Finally, all details of names and places are changed to protect confidentiality, unless otherwise specified by the submitting individual.

A special note of thanks to all those who have submitted texts, helped with translations and who otherwise contributed to this 2009 edition. It is our hope that this volume continues to be a service to all who work in the ministry of justice in the Church.

Contributions may be sent to the Office of the Executive Coordinator of the Canon Law Society of America.

Sr. Sharon Euart, RSM
Editor, *Roman Replies*
Office of the Executive Coordinator
3025 Fourth Street, NE
Hecker Center, Suite 111
Washington, DC 20017-1102

CANON 56 AND *SACRAMENTORUM SANCTITATIS TUTELA*

NOTIFICATION OF PRIEST OF DISPENSATION FROM PRIESTLY OBLIGATIONS INCLUDING CELIBACY

The Holy Father granted the petition for dispensation from celibacy and all obligations connected with ordination to the priesthood for a priest incardinated in a diocese of the United States. The voluntary petition was sent to the Congregation for the Doctrine of the Faith in accord with the provisions of Sacramentorum sanctitatis tutela. *The diocesan bishop attempted several times and by various means to notify the priest of the dispensation. The priest refused to respond to all efforts of the diocesan bishop to contact him. After a lengthy process, numerous efforts and significant cost to the diocese, the diocesan bishop contacted the Congregation for the Doctrine of the Faith. The correspondence between the Congregation for the Doctrine of the Faith and the bishop follows.*

Congregation for the Doctrine of the Faith [Unofficial Translation]
August 26, 2008

Reverend _____, a presbyter of the Archdiocese of _____, has humbly petitioned for a dispensation from sacred celibacy and from all the obligations connected with sacred ordination.

Our Most Holy Father, Benedict XVI, on August 26, 2008, after having received a report on the case from the Congregation for the Doctrine of the Faith, has granted the request, but with the following provisions:

1. The rescript of the dispensation, being made known by the competent Ordinary to the petitioner as soon as possible:
    a. *becomes effective from the moment of the notification;*
    b. *inseparably includes a dispensation from sacred celibacy and, at the same time, loss of the clerical state. The petitioner never has the right to separate those two elements, that is, to accept the first and refuse the second;*

c. *if the petitioner is a religious, the rescript also grants a dispensation from the vows;*
d. *indeed, further, it carries with it, insofar as it is necessary, absolution from censures.*

2. Notification of the dispensation can be made to the petitioner either personally, or through one delegated by the same Ordinary, or through an ecclesiastical notary, or by "registered mail." The Ordinary ought to retain one copy (of the rescript) duly signed by the petitioner in testimony of his reception of the rescript of the dispensation, and also of his acceptance of its regulations.

3. Notice of the granting of the dispensation is to be inscribed in the baptismal register of the petitioner's parish.

4. With regard to the celebration of a canonical marriage, the norms set down in The Code of Canon Law must be applied. The Ordinary, however, should take care that the matter be discreetly handled without pomp or external display.

5. The ecclesiastical authority, to whom it belongs to notify the petitioner concerning the rescript, should earnestly exhort him to take part in the life of the People of God, in a manner consonant with his new mode of living, to give edification, and thus to show himself a most loving son of the Church. At the same time, however, he should be informed of the following points:
   a. *the dispensed presbyter automatically loses the rights proper to the clerical state, as well as ecclesiastical dignities and offices; he is no longer bound by the other obligations connected with the clerical state;*
   b. *he remains excluded from the exercise of the sacred ministry, with the exception of those functions mentioned in canons 976 and 986, §2, and, as a result, he may not give a homily nor is he able to hold a directive office in the pastoral field nor to exercise the function of parochial administrator;*
   c. *similarly, he may not discharge any function in seminaries and in equivalent institutions. In other institutions of higher*

studies, which are in any way whatever dependent upon ecclesiastical authority, he may not exercise the function of director;

d. *however, in those institutions of higher studies which are not dependent upon ecclesiastical authority, he may not teach any discipline which is properly theological or closely connected with the same;*

e. *on the other hand, in institutions of lower studies, which are dependent upon ecclesiastical authority, he may not exercise the function of teaching a discipline which is properly theological. A dispensed presbyter is held by the same rule in teaching Religion in an institution of the same kind not dependent upon ecclesiastical authority;*

6. The Ordinary takes care, as much as possibly that the new condition of the dispended priest not show itself to be a scandal to the faithful. But, if the danger of abusing minors is present, the Ordinary can divulge the fact of the dispensation and the canonical cause.

7. At an opportune time, however, the competent Ordinary is to send a brief report to the Congregation on his completion of the notification, and, finally, if there should be any wonderment on the part of the faithful, he is to provide a prudent explanation.

All things to the contrary notwithstanding.

(signed) William Cardinal Leveda
Prefect

(signed) Aloisius F. Ladaria, S.J.
Archbishop Secretary

Bishop's communication to the Congregation for the Doctrine of the Faith outlining his attempts to contact the priest

---

February 2, 2009

Your Eminence:

In a rescript dated August 26, 2008, the Holy Father granted the petition of the Reverend _____ for dispensation from celibacy and all the obligations connected with ordination to the Priesthood. In accordance with the instructions of that rescript, I have made wide-ranging efforts to notify _____ of the rescript, to no avail.

My initial attempt was with a letter, sent through the US Postal Service by registered mail on September 22, 2008, asking him to meet with me so I could make the official notification personally. The letter was eventually returned to my office on October 11, 2008, marked "unclaimed," even though it was sent to the same address to which his sustenance payments were being sent. At that juncture, I suspended all sustenance payments since I could not longer verify that they were actually being received by the Reverend _____.

I next appointed as an ecclesiastical notary a private investigator, _____, to travel to the address of record in ___, in order to serve the notification on the Reverend _____. Mr. _____ learned that by then he had moved to _____, _____, South America.

Simultaneously, the Archdiocese of _____ received a subpoena from the US Department of Justice, Drug Enforcement Administration [DEA], seeking information about _____ in conjunction with what seems to be an investigation into money laundering connected with drug trafficking.

I thereupon directed _____ (ecclesiastical notary) to travel to _____ to serve the rescript on the Reverend _____. Upon advice from some contacts within the DEA, Mr. _____ made arrangements to have armed security accompany him during his visit to ____. He also had another person, General _____, make inquiries about the address which he has obtained as the residence in _____ for the Reverend _____. General _____ confirmed that he appeared to be living at that address.

Mr. _____'s efforts to deliver the rescript personally to the Reverend _____ are detailed in the accompanying report from the _____, Inc. I might also add that the Archdiocese has expended in excess of $25,000 USD in this effort to date.

The final communication from the Reverend _____'s sister was that he would travel to _____ to meet me, accompanied by her [she is also an attorney], and they would call to set up an appointment. I have waited approximately one month since that last communication. During this past week, I received a telephone call from the Reverend _____ about such an appointment and I have waited since then for the promised communication to no avail.

The conduct on his part is quite consistent with his earlier actions. He initially agreed to seek laicization voluntarily, then later changed his mind. When my predecessor told him that he would institute a petition to C.D.F. requesting that he be deposed from the clerical state he again agreed to the voluntary petition. Following my appointment to the Archdiocese of _____ he indicated he did not wish to pursue the petition and actually wrote to the Congregation for Clergy asking assistance to remain in the priesthood. I advised the Congregation of the petition then pending at C.D.F. and informed the Reverend _____ of that correspondence and of my determination to adopt the same approach as my predecessor. He then agreed once again to pursue the voluntary petition.

It is my opinion that the Reverend _____ is using the present tactic as a method of stalling, and preventing the rescript from becoming active. This is further displayed by the most recent telephone call he made to my office, indicating that he would have his civil attorney make contact with me. That still has not ensued.

In the file which I forwarded to the Congregation regarding his original petition, I detailed the reasons why it is imperative that the Reverend _____ should never be returned to active ministry and why his reduction to the lay state is critically important and urgent. The interest of the DEA regarding possible civil criminal violations only adds urgency to my request.

Given his refusal to accept notification of the rescript, I now humbly seek your advice.

My original letter asking him to meet with me indicated that I had received an answer from the Holy See regarding his petition and that I needed to meet with him in connection with that decree to make arrangements to fulfill my predecessor's promise for financial assistance for him to transition to the lay state. The same message was included in my letter of October 16, 2008, which was given to Mr. _____ (ecclesial notary) to hand-deliver to the Reverend _____.

The Reverend _____'s telephone conversations with Mr. _____ make it clear that he is aware I am trying to get documents to him pertaining to his petition for laicization. The report also shows that a Fr. _____ tried to persuade him to accept the notification.

Given all the circumstances mentioned above, I propose three possibilities to resolve the matter:

1) Can this refusal be taken as analogous to the provision of canon 1510 whereby a person "who refuses to accept the document of citation or who prevents its arrival is considered as having been legitimately cited."
2) If the answer to that question is negative, can the rescript now be made effective without the notification having been attained?

If neither of the above is possible, can we simply convert it to an administrative process for involuntary laicization, using the materials already in the file sent to C.D.F., given that he has already admitted to his pervasive sexual activities with both men and women over the course of his entire priesthood, and did not deny the accusation of child molestation in the case of one individual who finally came forward when he heard that the Reverend _____ was trying to return to active ministry?

If any one of the above can be answered in the affirmative, it will resolve more easily what is potentially a very dangerous situation for the Archdiocese.

I am enclosing as additional material for your consideration the report from _____, Inc.; a copy of the letter which was sent to him and which he refused to accept; a copy of the decree of appointment of Mr. _____ as an ecclesiastical notary and a copy of the subpoena from the Drug Enforcement Administration.

Your Eminence, I thank you for your kind assistance and direction in this matter.

Fraternally in Christ,

(signed) Archbishop of _____

Congregation for the Doctrine of the Faith
February 23, 2009
Confidential

Your Excellency,

The Congregation for the Doctrine of the Faith received, on 6 February 2009, your correspondence regarding Mr. _____ to whom Pope Benedict XVI granted, on 26 August 2008, the grace of dispensation from all priestly obligations, including celibacy.

This Dicastery, after a careful and attentive study of the facts presented, including the account of your extraordinary effort to communicate the Decree of the Holy Father to Mr. _____, decided that

> The Ponifical Rescript of His Holiness Pope Benedict XVI dated 26 August 2008, CDF Prot. No. ___, has been properly communicated according to the norms of can. 56, *CIC* 1983

Given the seriousness of this matter, His Eminence_____, Archbishop of _____, The Episcopal Conference of _____, and the United States Conference of Catholic Bishops should be promptly notified about the canonical status of Mr. _____.

./..

Furthermore, Your Excellency should notify the Ordinary of the Diocese where Mr. _____'s baptism took place. As specified in the paragraph 3 of the Decree, the fact that he was dispensed from all the obligations connected with sacred ordination and lost the clerical state should be inscribed in his baptismal record.

With gratitude for your assistance in this serious matter and prayerful best wishes, I remain,

Sincerely yours in Christ,

(signed)

Canon 76

CONFERRAL OF PONTIFICAL HONORS

In 2001, the Vatican Secretariat of State issued an Instruction on the Conferral of Pontifical Honors outlining the procedures for such recognition of clergy and laity. The text of the Instruction follows:

Apostolic Nunciature
United States of America
June 19, 2001
N.10.837

Your Eminences and Your Excellencies,

At the direction of the Secretariat of State of His Holiness, I have the honor to transmit to you, distinguished Diocesan Ordinaries, an English translation of the new Instruction on the Conferral of Pontifical Honors (Prot. 16.846/ON), signed by His Eminence Angelo Cardinal Sodano, Secretary of State of His Holiness, on May 13, 2001.

Thanking your for your kind attention in this matter, in particular on the special occasions when you choose to honor those deserving of such papal recognition, I remain, with cordial regards and prayerful best wishes,

Sincerely, yours in Christ,

(signed) Archbishop Gabriel Montalvo
Apostolic Nuncio

Secretariat of State

Instruction on the Conferral of Pontifical Honors
May 13, 2001
Prot. No. 16.846/ON

The Diocesan Bishops are able to propose the conferral of a pontifical honor upon ecclesiastics and the laity, as a sign of appreciation and recognition of the service they have rendered. Likewise, a Vicar General is able to request such a conferral, however, declaring explicitly that he is proceeding in this regard with the expressed authorization of the proper Bishop.

The request, accompanied by the *"curriculum vitae"* of the candidate(s) *(year of age, profession, family and social condition; with an accurate description of the worthwhile merits of the candidate with respect to the Church)*, must be sent to the Apostolic Nunciature, which, having given its *nihil obstat*, will forward said request(s) to the Secretariat of State of His Holiness. Petitions being made by those territories subject to the jurisdiction of the Congregations for the Oriental Churches and the Evangelization of Peoples should first be addressed always through the Apostolic Nunciature, to the respective competent Dicastery, which, in turn, will forward such to the Secretariat of State of His Holiness.

1-Secular Clergy:

a) *Chaplain to His Holiness*: to priests who are at least 35 years old and have been a priest for 10 years;
b) *Prelate of Honor to His Holiness*: to priests who are at least 45 years old and have been a priest for 15 years;
c) *Protonotary Apostolic Supernumerary*: to priests who are at least 55 years old and have been a priest for 20 years;
d) The norm of graduality must be observed: i.e., a given candidate must have first the title of Chaplain to His Holiness, and then that of Prelate of Honor to His Holiness. From this grade to another a period of at least 10 years ought to pass.
e) For some cases of particular and significant merit, the Bishops are able to request directly the title of Protonotary Apostolic Supernumerary, while preserving the condition that the candidate is at lease 55 years old and ordained a priest for 20 years.
f) For each Diocese, the total number of Chaplains, Prelates and Protonotaries ought not to exceed ten percent of the clergy.

2-*Religious Men and Women*

For Religious men and women, after a noteworthy period of service, the honorary distinctions of the *Benemerenti* Medal and the *Pro Ecclesia et Pontifice* Cross may be requested:

a) **Benemerenti Medal**: to candidates who are at least 35 years old and who have completed 10 years of religious profession.
b) **Pro Ecclesia et Pontifice Cross**: to candidates who are at least 45 years old and who have completed 15 years of religious profession.

3- The Laity

For the laity, men and women, the Equestrian Orders presently conferred are the Pian Order, the Order of St. Gregory the Great and the Order of Pope St. Silvester in the degrees of Knights and Dames of the Collar (only for the Pian Order); Knights and Dames of Grand Cross; Commanders with Star and Dames (Dame di Commenda) with Star, Commanders and Dames (Dame di Commenda); Knights and Dames. Together with the Equestrian Orders exist also, as distinctions of honor, the *Benemerenti* Medal and the *Pro Ecclesia et Pontifice* Cross. The Supreme Order of Christ and the Order of the Golden Spur, although not abolished, are presently not under consideration.

I. Pian Order

a) ***The Collar***: is granted to Heads of State
b) ***The Grand Cross***: to Heads of Government, Ministers of State and Ambassadors accredited to the Holy See.

II. Order of St. Gregory the Great

a) ***Grand Cross***: to candidates of high profile in the service of the Church, at national and international levels, who are at least 55 years old and 10 years after the conferral of an honor of inferior degree.
b) ***Commander with Star***: to candidates particularly well-deserving, who are at least 45 years old and 10 years after the conferral of an honor of inferior degree.
c) ***Commander***: to candidates well-deserving, who are at least 45 years old and 10 years after the conferral of an honor of inferior degree.
d) ***Knighthood***: to candidates who are at least 40 years old.

III. Order of Pope St. Silvester

a) ***Grand Cross***: to candidates particularly well-deserving, who are at least 50 years old and 10 years after the conferral of an honor of inferior degree.

b) ***Commander with Star***: to candidates well-deserving, who are at least 45 years old and 10 years after the conferral of an honor of inferior degree.
c) ***Commander***: to candidates who are at least 40 years old and 10 years after the conferral of an honor of inferior degree.
d) ***Knighthood***: to candidates who are at least 35 years old.

IV. The Benemerenti Medal and the Pro Ecclesia et Pontifice Cross

a) It is possible to request also for the laity (men and women) the *Benemerenti* Medal and the *Pro Ecclesia et Pontifice* Cross with the same conditions established for Religious, men and women, that is 35 years old for the *Benemerenti* Medal and 45 years old for the *Pro Ecclesia et Pontifice* Cross.
b) Also in this case, the criteria of graduality is to be respected as established for ecclesiastics.

4- Police and Military Forces in General:

a) The honors are conferred only to those who have the rank of Captain and higher ranks. Hence, the request for Warrant Officers, Under-lieutenants, and Lieutenants is to be avoided.
b) To Captains, Captains major and Majors is granted the Order of Pope St. Silvester; to Lieutenant-Colonels, Colonels and Generals the Order of St. Gregory the Great, in various degrees.

5- For Nominations from Within the Roman Curia

The proposal of the conferral of a pontifical honor for the Official(s) of the Roman Curia (Secular clergy, Religious men and women, the Laity) ought to be presented to the Secretariat of State of His Holiness by his or her proper head of dicastery, together with a detailed *"curriculum vitae"* of the candidate.

(signed) Angelo Cardinal Sodano
Secretary of State

Secretariat of State
Clarification Regarding Papal Honors
Prot. No. 17.567/ON

1- For Clerics:

a) The Holy See alone has exclusive authority to grand honorary titles, with respect, of course, for the traditions of the Oriental Churches (cf. *CCEO*, c. 250).

b) To respect graduality, every candidate (of any age or merit) is given first the title of Chaplain to His Holiness, and only this title.

c) However, the title of Prelate of Honor to His Holiness can be granted as a first step, upon request of the diocesan Bishop, to Vicars General who are not religious.

d) Only in exceptional cases, and with a well-documented request from the Ordinary, can the concession of the title of Prelate of Honor to His Holiness be considered as a first step for a cleric who is not a Vicar General, but who should be advanced in years (e.g., 75 years old) and be truly deserving of said honor.

e) The same holds true with greater reason for the title of Protonotary Apostolic Supernumerary.

f) For all candidates an interval of 10 years must be observed between on Honor and another.

2- For Laity:

a) The concession of Honors *must* be regulated by the principle of graduality.

b) As a *first step*, all will be granted the Knighthood of the Order of Pope St. Silvester and the Order of St. Gregory the Great, depending on the age of the candidate (dv. Instruction of May 13, 2001 [p.n. 16.846/ON], 3, II and III).

c) To candidates who are particularly deserving, and whose merits are adequately documented by the Diocesan Ordinary, the rank of Commander and the Commander with Star of the two Orders can be conferred *first*, depending on the age of each (cf. *ibidem*).

d) The concession of the Grand Cross of both Orders is to be considered truly exceptional.

e) For all candidates an interval of 10 years must be observed between one Honor and another.

3- In All Cases

It sometimes happens that Bishops request a rather elevated number of Honors on the occasion of particular celebrations. In this regard, the following is to be kept clearly in mind:

a) For every diocese, the total number of Protonotaries, Prelates and Chaplains *must* not exceed 10% of the clergy.
b) For the laity, no diocese can request more than 10 Honors per year for each of the Orders of Pope St. Silvester and St. Gregory the Great.
c) The *Benemerenti* Medals and the *Pro Ecclesia et Pontifice* crosses cannot be more than 20 per year per diocese.

Canons 180-183

REQUEST FOR DISPENSATION FOR POSSIBLE POSTULATION

A major superior sought an indult from the Congregation for Institutes of Consecrated Life and Societies of Apostolic Life (CICLSAL) prior to institute's Chapter for the possible postulation of members who had already served the two terms in general government permitted by the institute's Constitutions. The Holy See's response reminded the superior of the requirements for a valid postulation and indicated that a dispensation could not be granted in advance of the election. The response of the CICLSAL follows:

Congregation for Institutes of Consecrated Life and Societies of Apostolic Life
January 23, 2008

Dear Sister _______,

This letter comes in response to yours of 4 January 2008, regarding the General Chapter of the _____, scheduled for _____, 2008. You have asked how to proceed in the face of the possible postulation of members of the General Government who have already served the two terms permitted by your Constitutions.

While this is an impediment which can be dispensed, in order to leave the Chapter fully free, it is not the practice of this Dicastery to grant a dispensation in elections before the Chapter. In the event that there is the postulation of any of these persons, according to the canonical norms (cc. 180-183), it can be sent to us immediately by fax, and we will make every effort ot respond the next day. With the time difference, your fax would arrive when we are closed on March 31, but we would have the full day on April 1 to reach you during your day.

In cases of postulation, it is important to include that it took place on the first or second ballot, that there was the necessary 2/3 vote for postulation, and to indicate again briefly the reasons for postulation. The person who is presiding during the election, and/or Bishop _____, can forward the request. It will facilitate the matter also to make reference to the above protocol number.

With personal best wishes and prayer for the Holy Spirit's light and strength as you prepare for and celebrate your Chapter, I remain

Yours sincerely in Christ,

(signed) Undersecretary

Canon 616, §4

SUPPRESSION OF A *SUI IURIS* MONASTERY OF NUNS

A diocesan bishop learned from his vicar for religious that a sui iuris *monastery in the diocese had five nuns in their eighties, three of whom were infirm. The vicar reported that during his annual visitations to the monastery, he repeatedly requested that the nuns look to their future and plan for the suppression of the monastery, since the infirm nuns needed provision for assisted living and no vocations were forthcoming for a number of years. However, the nuns refused to take any steps towards the suppression of the monastery and providing for their own retirement needs. The bishop took recourse to the Congregation for Institutes of Consecrated Life and Societies of Apostolic Life (CICLSAL) and received the following response:*

Congregation for Institutes of Consecrated Life and Societies of Apostolic Life

Decree

The Congregation for Institutes of Consecrated Life and Societies of Apostolic Life, because of the declining number of Nuns and the difficulty for the aging Community, with this present Decree decides to suppress the Monastery of _____ in the diocese of _____.

The Nuns must move to other Monasteries of the same Order, which will be ready to accept them with the same rights and duties which the Nuns enjoyed in their Monastery.

Pious legacies, if there be any, must be used for the purpose intended by the donor or testator; likewise, the rights of others, if there be any, must be preserved intact insofar as the case demands.

It pertains to the Bishop of _____ to execute this Decree and to inform this Congregation about its execution.

All things to the contrary notwithstanding.

(signed) Secretary
(signed) Undersecretary

The bishop of the diocese where the monastery was located issued the following decree:

Decree

I, the undersigned bishop of _____, having received the Decree (Prot. N. _) of the Congregation for Institutes of Consecrated Life and Societies of Apostolic Life, suppressing the Monastery of the Sisters of _____, in the diocese of _____, have examined it and judge it to be authentic. Having been entrusted by the same Congregation with the Decree's execution, I do hereby execute it in conformity with the provisions of canon 41 of the Code of Canon Law.

In conformity with the provision of canon 54 §1, the decree takes effect immediately.

All things to the contrary notwithstanding.

Given in _____ at the Curia of the _____, _____(date).

(signed) Chancellor
(signed) Bishop of _____

Canon 667, §3 and *Verbi Sponsa*

PERMISSION FOR ABSENCE FOR THE DURATION OF NECESSITY FOR A CONTEMPLATIVE NUN

A nun, an only child, in solemn profession in a sui iuris *monastery was granted permission to live apart from the monastery for three months by the diocesan bishop where the monastery was located to take care of her ill mother in accord with the instruction* Verbi Sponsa *17 §2 of the Congregation for Institutes of Consecrated Life and Societies of Apostolic Life (CICLSAL). The nun's mother became critical and was placed on oxygen and other life-sustaining supports. CICLSAL extended the permission to live apart from the monastery to the nun for one year. Since her mother continued in the critical condition at the end of the year, the superior of the monastery petitioned CICLSAL for a second extension of the permission. The following rescript was received from CICLSAL:*

Congregation for Institutes of Consecrated Life and Societies of Apostolic Life

Most Holy Father,

Sister _____, a solemnly professed member of the Monastery of _____, _____, diocese of _____, requests of your Holiness an extension of the permission, Prot. N. __, issued on _____ for the reasons presented.

The Congregation for Institutes of Consecrated Life and Societies of Apostolic Life, after careful consideration of the reason presented, grants the faculty to the Superior of the Monastery to concede the permission of absence to Sister _____, for the time that she considers necessary. All other provisions of the law are to be observed.

All things to the contrary notwithstanding.

(signed) Undersecretary
(signed) Prefect

CANON 702

SUPPORT FOR A SEPARATED MEMBER OF A RELIGIOUS INSTITUTE

Upon departure from her religious institute, a woman was given assistance that the general superior and council considered appropriate in light of the canonical requirement to "observe equity and charity" (c. 702) towards a member who is separated from it. The former member did not consider the assistance the institute offered sufficient for her life style and asked the Congregation for Institutes of Consecrated Life and Societies of Apostolic Life (CICLSAL) to intervene on her behalf. The Congregation responded to the departing member communicating that any decision regarding additional assistance to her would be determined by the superior and the council. The text of the Congregation's response follows:

Congregation for Institutes of Consecrated Life and Societies of Apostolic Life
January 21, 2008

Dear Sr. _____,

Your letter of December 21, 2007, regarding the support offered to _____ upon her departure from your Institute, has been received in this Congregation for Institutes of Consecrated Life and Societies of Apostolic Life. Thank you for having forwarded this information.

In our original correspondence with Miss _____, this Dicastery clearly communicated that any decision regarding additional assistance would be decided upon by you and your Council.

We are satisfied to learn that the matter was reconsidered and that, following consultation with your Council and other advisors, you have arrived at the conclusion that "*additional assistance at this time is unwarranted.*" We were also pleased to note your openness to offer further assistance in the future based on Miss _____'s "*demonstrated need.*"

May the Lord abundantly bless you, your Council and all the ____ Sisters.
Sincerely in Christ,

(signed) Undersecretary

CANON 903 (CIC) AND CANON 703, §1 (CCEO) AND *ESSENTIAL NORMS FOR DIOCESAN/EPARCHIAL POLICIES DEALING WITH ALLEGATIONS OF SEXUAL ABUSE OF MINORS BY PRIESTS AND DEACONS*

LETTERS/STATEMENTS ON SUITABILITY OF PRIESTS FOR PUBLIC MINISTRY

The USCCB Committee for the Protection of Children and Young People was asked to provide model letters on: 1) the suitability of a religious priest for a stable assignment in a diocese; 2) the suitability for temporary ministry of religious priests; and 3) a celebret or testimonial letter acknowledging a diocesan priest's suitability for ministry. Following discussion by the USCCB Committee for the Protection of Children and Young People (CPCYP) and in consultation with the USCCB Committee on Canonical Affairs and Church Governance, the following texts were offered to the bishops in October 2008 as models for accepting a priest into the diocese or eparchy for public ministry in fulfillment of Norm 12 of Essential Norms. *The text of the suitability letters follows:*

United States Conference of Catholic Bishops
Committee for the Protection of Children and Young People
October 31, 2008

The Bishop's Committee for the Protection of Children and Young People was asked to provide model letters on the following:

1. The suitability of a religious priest for a stable assignment in a diocese
2. The suitability for temporary ministry of religious priests
3. A model for a celebret or testimonial letter acknowledging a diocesan priest's suitability for ministry

After thorough discussion by the Committee for the Protection of Children and Young People and in consultation with the Bishops' Committee on Canonical Affairs and Church Governance, I present these models to you confident that they provide the essential information that a diocesan bishop or eparch needs in order to accept a priest into the diocese or eparchy for public ministry.

Some documents that are circulating at the present time seem to be excessive in details and others seem to be vague. The CPCYP has studied the attached documents carefully and presents them to you for possible use in the United States.

The USCCB has no authority to require that a specific form of a *celebret* or other authorization be used. Rather, these texts are offered simply as models for consideration when implementing Church law on a local level.

Thank you for your continued support. If you have any questions or comments, please do not hesitate to contact Ms. Teresa Kettelkamp at the Secretariat of Child and Youth Protection at (202) 541-5413 / tkettelkamp@usccb.org or Msgr. Ronny Jenkins, Associate General Secretary at (202) 541-3100 / rjenkins@usccb.org.

(signed) Most Reverend Gregory M. Aymond
Chair

Model for a Letter/Statement on the Suitability of a Religious Priest for a Stable Assignment

Dear (Arch)Bishop N.N.:

Under the Guidelines proposed by the United States Conference of Catholic Bishops, Conference of Major Superiors of Men, Leadership Conference of Women Religious and Council of Major Superiors of Women Religious (NCCB, November 1993) and the policies of this religious institute, I write to certify the suitability of [NAME] as a member of this religious institute in good standing. I do this in the spirit of mutuality, trust, respect and common understanding in accord with the principles set for in *Mutuae Relationes* (Rome, May 14, 1978).

Specifically, I write to inform you that I have proposed a member of our Province, Rev. [NAME], to the [PLACE], effective [DATE], as [ASSIGNMENT].

[NAME] was born on [DATE], made his Final Profession on [DATE], and was ordained to the Priesthood on [DATE]. [Include information such as

DATES OF PREVIOUS ASSIGNMENTS, RELEVANT INFORMATION, and SPECIAL SKILLS here].

I am able to the best of my ability to assure you that [NAME] is a person of good moral character and reputation and is qualified to serve in an effective and suitable manner in your diocese. In addition, also based on inquiry and to the best of my knowledge, and in light of the provisions of can. 903 *CIC* and can. 703 §1 *CCEO*, I can assure you that nothing in his background in anyway would limit or disqualify him from this assignment.

I am unaware of anything in his background which would render him unsuitable to work with minor children. [NAME] has completed training in an educational program, a diocesan and/or the CMSM *Instruments of Hope and Healing-Safeguarding Children and Young People* program, conducted by Praesidium Religious Services, [GIVE DATES OF ATTENDANCE], which is in accord with the *Essential Norms for Diocesan/Eparchial Policies Dealing with Allegations of Sexual Abuse of Minors by Priests and Deacons* (USCCB 2006).

Therefore, I respectfully ask that the priestly faculties of the [NAME OF (ARCH)DIOCESE or EPARCHY] be granted to [NAME], effective [DATE], and for the duration of his assignment to [PLACE].

Be assured of my prayers for you during this time.

Respectfully in Christ,

[Name of the Major Superior]
[Title]
[Date]
Effective _________ through ___________

Model for a Celebret/Testimonial of Suitability for Temporary Ministry of Religious Priests

Dear (Arch)Bishop N.N.:

In light of the provisions of can. 903 *CIC* and can. 703 §1 *CCEO*, and under the Guidelines proposed by the United States Conference of Catholic Bishops, Conference of Major Superiors of Men, Leadership Conference of Women Religious and Council of Major Superiors of Women Religious

(NCCB, November 1993) and the policies of this religious institute, I write to certify the suitability of [NAME] as a member of this religious institute in good standing. I do this in the spirit of mutuality, trust, respect and common understanding in accord with the principles set forth in *Mutuae Relationes* (Rome, May 14, 1978).

Specifically, I write to inform you that Rev. [NAME] is a member of the Province of [PROVINCE NAME], who currently resides in [PLACE OF RESIDENCE]. He will be exercising ministry at [NAME OF THE CHURCH OR INSTITUTION] in [LOCATION OF THE CHURCH OR INSTITUTION] in your diocese, on [DATE].

I am able to make the following statements:

- He is a person of good moral character and reputation.
- I know nothing which would in any way limit or disqualify him from this ministry.
- I am unaware of anything in his background which would render him unsuitable to work with minor children.

Respectfully in Christ,

[Name of the (Arch)bishop/Eparch]
[Title]
[Date]
Effective ______________ through ______________

Model for a Celebret/Testimonial of Suitability for Temporary Ministry of Diocesan Priests

Dear (Arch)Bishop N.N.:

In light of the provisions of can. 903 *CIC* and can. 703, §1 *CCEO*, I write to inform you that Rev. [NAME] is an incardinated priest of the [(Arch)diocese/Eparchy] of [LOCATION], who currently resides in [PLACE OF RESIDENCE]. He will be exercising ministry at [NAME OF THE CHURCH OR INSTITUTION] in [LOCATION OF THE CHURCH OR INSTITUTION] in your diocese, on [DATE].

In regard to Rev. [NAME], I am able to make the following statements:

- He is a person of good moral character and reputation.

- I know nothing which would in any way limit or disqualify him from this ministry.
- I am unaware of anything in his background which would render him unsuitable to work with minor children.

Respectfully in Christ,

[Name of the (Arch)bishop/Eparch]
[Title]
[Date]
Effective ___________ through ______________

CANONS 1061, 1681, 1704§1

REQUESTS FOR DISPENSATION OF A *RATUM ET NON CONSUMMATUM* MARRIAGE

In a memorandum to the U.S. Bishops dated August 3, 2009, Cardinal Francis George, O.M.I., President of the United States Conference of Catholic Bishops, forwarded a request from His Eminence Cardinal Antonio Cañizares Llovera, Prefect of the Congregation for Divine Worship and the Discipline of the Sacraments, dated June 13, 2009 (Port. N. 551/09M), that the Congregation's December 20, 1986 procedures be disseminated to those competent in such matters. An English translation of the 1986 procedures can be found in Canon Law Digest Vol. 13, pages 695-701. The Congregation expressed concern that some tribunal officials, viewing the ratum *process as highly specialized and complex, may be hesitant to utilize it, even in appropriate cases. To assist with the local instruction of such cases and the preparation of the necessary* acta *for submission to the Holy See, the Congregation also provided a helpful* Pro Memoria. *An English translation of the* Pro Memoria, *prepared by USCCB staff, follows:*

Congregation for Divine Worship and Discipline of the Sacraments
June 13, 2009
(*unofficial translation*)

Pro Memoria

For the Instruction of a Cause for Dispensation of a Ratum et Non Consummatum Marriage

1. The petition of both spouses, or of one of the two, is directed to the Holy Father, with a summary of the matrimonial history, an indication of the causes that have prevented the consummation, the reasons for the dispensation being sought, the date and place of the drafting of the *libellus*, and the diocese of the domicile or quasi-domicile of the one, or both, petitioner(s).
2. The request ought to be signed by hand.
3. The pastoral attempts to obtain the reconciliation of the parties ought to appear in the acts.
4. The baptismal certificates of the parties and the marriage certificate (original copies). Birth certificates of children conceived before the marriage.

5. If applicable, the acts of a civil process of divorce, separation or nullity; or at least copies of the sentence of the civil Tribunal.

6. The decrees of appointment of the Instructor of the cause, thc Defender of the Bond and the Notary. The instructing judge, which in a first instance Tribunal will be a single judge, must always to be a priest (*semper debet esse sacerdos*), who can rely, in case of necessity, on a lay person, but as an auditor only (*tantum uti auditor*).

7. The interrogation of the parties is to be conducted by the Instructor in the presence of the Notary and the Defender of the Bond, under oath to speak the truth (*de veritate dicenda*), with questions designed to clarify the marriage of the parties and, at the conclusion, under oath confirming the truth of what was said (*de veritate dictorum*). In particularly delicate or complex cases involving the manner of intimate life, a medical expert may be present to pose the questions.

8. Include, if applicable, the acts of a canonical trial for the declaration of nullity of marriage.

9. For the suspension of the process of nullity, the consent of the parties (*consensus partium*) is required by can. 1681. However, if the respondent was declared absent by the judge during the cause of nullity, he or she must be cited for the purpose of obtaining consent regarding the transfer of the cause to the administrative process. Bearing in mind can. 1592 §1 and *Dignitas Connubii* 138 §3, if the respondent, legitimately cited, does not respond to the citation, the tribunal may interpret this silence as a tacit assent to the suspension of the process and to the procedure for requesting the dispensation.

10. The interrogation of witnesses, indicated by the parties or selected by the Instructor, under oath to speak the truth (*de veritate dicenda*), is to be conducted with prepared questions, pertaining to their knowledge of the non-consummation and of the more significant aspects of the case.

11. Collect attestations of the credibility of the parties and of the witnesses from their pastors or, in their absence, from other priests, religious or committed laity who have particular knowledge of the persons in the case.

12. Enclose any medical examinations on the state of the genital organs of the woman, of the man, and on their capacity or not for conjugal life, and other aspects relative to the case.

13. Enclose other useful documents for physical and moral proofs (for example, medical records, police reports, private letters, etc.).

14. A suitable report (*apta relatio*) from the Instructor providing a summary of the process (cf. can. 1704 §1).

15. The animadversions of the Defender of the Bond with the grounds for reasonably (*rationabiliter*) opposing the dispensation of the marriage (cf. cann. 1432 and 1701 §1).

16. The votum of the Bishop of the domicile or quasi-domicile of the petitioner, *pro rei veritate* guaranteeing the absence of scandal from the granting of the dispensation (cf. can. 1704 §1 CIC and art. 23 of the Circular Letter of the Congregation for the Sacraments of December 20, 1986).

17. The above acts, written or translated exclusively in a language used by the Roman Curia (Latin, Italian, Spanish, Portuguese, French, English, German), collected and neatly bound, arranged and numbered, with an index, should all be authenticated by a Notary, and shipped in triplicate copy to the Congregation for Divine Worship and the Discipline of the Sacraments, and not containing illegible handwritten documents, which, if deemed of any importance, must be transcribed into typewriting. This applies equally to the legibility of photocopies. Also note that the original acts of the proceedings must be kept in the archive of the diocesan curia.

18. The Congregation is always sensitive to the inclusion of a request for a reduction in fees and, in more severe cases, even a total exemption, provided it is accompanied by documentation and a recommendation from the diocesan curia, which, in turn, declares its inability to cover the actual costs locally for the Congregation.

CANONS 1086, §1; 1117; 1124

CIRCULAR LETTER ON THE *ACTUS FORMALIS DEFECTIONIS AB ECCLESIA CATHOLICA* FROM THE PONTIFICAL COUNCIL FOR LEGISLATIVE TEXTS

Following the promulgation of the Circular Letter on the Actus Formalis Defectionis ab Ecclesia Catholica *by the Pontifical Council for Legislative Texts in March 2006, the Council received a request for further clarification on three points in the Circular Letter. The response of the Pontifical Council has been translated from the original Spanish and is as follows:*

Vatican City, December 16, 2006

Most Reverend Excellency:

It has arrived in time to this Pontifical Council your kind letter about the "Guidelines" approved by that Episcopal Conference on how to proceed in case of a request of formal abandonment of the Church, in relation to the Circular Letter of this Dicastery of March 13, 2006, Prot N. 10279/2006, in which you put three questions:

a) If, in light of the "Norms" of the Pontifical Council, the approach of processing applications of formal abandonment in the diocese of baptism can be maintained?
b) If, in light of the "Norms" of the Pontifical Council, the approach of managing the process by mail when the interested person refuses to appear can continue?
c) If, in light of the "Norms" of the Pontifical Council, the approach of centralizing the process in the diocesan curia can be maintained?

Above all it is a satisfaction to see that those "Guidelines", in anticipation of the Circular Letter of this Pontifical Council, had addressed this sensitive issue timely. The "Guidelines" also show the correct perception that only if the external manifestation is the consequence of an internal act of apostasy, heresy or schism, a proper formal act of rupture of ecclesiastical communion, with the subsequent consequence of the canonical penalty of excommunication (cf. cans. 751 and 1364), may exist.

As to the doubts raised by that Conference, its careful study has allowed the formulation of the following responses:

1. On the approach of processing the application. The rules of the Circular letter provide that the review of the application itself is undertaken by the proper Ordinary (diocesan Bishop, Vicar general or episcopal Vicar, if there is one) or the proper parish priest, which are those of the place of the domicile, quasi-domicile or place of residence (cf. can. 107). The reason for this attribution of competence is that it is easier for the ecclesiastical authority of the place of residence of the faithful to find him and establish with the faithful the necessary pastoral dialogue. The purpose of this personal dialogue is threefold: a) help him to become aware of the gravity of this act and of the resulting canonical penalty of excommunication; b) explain to him the consequences already transcribed in the n.4 (the 5th indent) of the "Guidelines"[1]; c) seek with patient charity his conversion and desist from his intention to abandon. If despite this pastoral dialogue the faithful insists in his petition the proper Ordinary or parish priest will communicate the decision itself, if it is a different diocese, to the diocese of Baptism, for entry in the appropriate parish book.

2. On the management of the procedure by mail. Failing to establish a convenient personal dialogue, it will also be possible to record the abandonment, and provide for its entry in the book of baptisms, when, through direct postal communication between the faithful and the proper Ordinary or parish priest, it is deemed to have fulfilled all the conditions of the formal act of abandonment. For that the ecclesiastical authority should state in the letter what he would have said to the faithful if a personal meeting would have been possible (n.2). The letter must be certified, as is already planned so accurately in the "Guidelines," because only if it is known that it has come to the faithful and he has confirmed with an expressed or implied answer his decision to abandon, the

---

[1] Transcript of the n. 4, 5th indent of the "Guidelines": [From the abandonment of the Catholic Church by formal act (that is, under canon law, an act of apostasy, heresy or schism)] "with the following consequences: Exclusion from the sacraments (cf. cc. 1331, §1, 2° and 915); Deprivation of ecclesiastical burial, unless before death the person would have given some sign of repentance (cf. c. 1184 §1, 1°); Exclusion of the possibility of being a godfather for the baptism and confirmation (cf. cc. 874, §1, 4° and 893, §1); Need for permission from the local Ordinary for admission to a canonical marriage (cf. c. 1071, §1, 5°)"

procedure can be completed communicating the decision, if it is a different diocese, to the diocese of Baptism.

3. About the centralization in the diocesan curia. The rules of the Holy See taking into account the diversity of situations by country left free to choose if the procedure is performed before the Ordinary or the pastor. As long as the necessary conditions for the existence of a formal act of abandonment as indicated in nn. 1 and 2 have been fulfilled it is left to the discretionary choice of the Episcopal Conference to centralize the procedure or not.

In the hope that these observations could be useful, I'm happy to take this opportunity to renew my sentiments of profound esteem and warm affection in Christ.

(signed) Julián Card. Herranz
President

(signed) Bruno Bertagna
Bishop Secretary

CANON 1292, §1

MAXIMUM AND MINIMUM SUMS FOR THE ALIENATION OF ECCLESIASTICAL GOODS

United States Conference of Catholic Bishops
Office of the President
May 21, 2009

Your Eminence/Excellency,

You will recall that on March 31, 2008, the Congregation for Bishops extended its *recognitio* of the USCCB's complementary norms to canon 1292 §1 CIC, concerning the maximum and minimum sums for the alienation of ecclesiastical goods. The complementary norms call for an annual adjustment of the sums according to the rate of inflation provided by the United States Bureau of Labor Statistics.

By means of this communication, and at the request of Most Reverend Thomas J. Paprocki, Chairman of the Committee on Canonical Affairs and Church Governance, I write to inform you that the adjusted sums for the maximum and minimum alienation of ecclesiastical goods, effective immediately, are as follows:

> Maximum: $11,397,000 for populations of 500,000 or more, $5,699,000 for all others (raised from $10,948,000 and $5,475,000 respectively),
> Minimum: $1,140,000 for populations of 500,000 or more, $570,000 for all others (raised from $1,095,000 and $547,500 respectively),
> For other juridical persons subject to the Diocesan Bishop the new maximum sum for alienation is $5,699,000 (raised from $5,475,000) and the minimum is $28,495 (from $27,373) or 5% of the prior year's ordinary annual income, whichever is greater.

I would be grateful if you would share this information with the appropriate personnel within your diocese. The new sums are also posted on the USCCB's website.

With hope that the above information will be helpful to you in your ongoing administration of temporal goods, and with assurances of my prayerful best wishes, I am

Fraternally yours in Christ,

(signed) Francis Cardinal George, OMI
President

Canons 1317; 1319; 1342, §2; 1349; 1399

SPECIAL FACULTIES FOR CONGREGATION FOR CLERGY
ADMINISTRATIVE PROCEDURE FOR THE LAICIZATION OF PRIESTS

Pope Benedict XVI granted the Congregation for Clergy three special faculties for dismissal of clerics from the priesthood and the obligations of celibacy in certain circumstances. The faculties provide additional means not available in the Code of Canon Law to resolve grave violations of clerical celibacy or situations where clerics have abandoned their ministry for an extended period of time. The text of the Circular Letter of the Congregation for the Clergy[1] *follows:*

Congregation for Clergy
April 18, 2009

Your Eminence, Your Excellency,

Last Jan. 30 the supreme pontiff granted certain special faculties to this congregation. The purpose of this circular letter is to present these faculties to all ordinaries so that the reasoning behind them and the ends which they seek to accomplish are clearly understood in the manner in which they were originally intended.

The congregation was moved to write this letter to the most reverend ordinaries by virtue of its ardent desire to honor the mission and person of those priests who, faithful to their authentic priestly identity and mission, think, act and live in a countercultural manner in this heavily secularized moment in history, as well as to assist the successors of the apostles in their daily task of preserving and promoting ecclesiastical discipline for the benefit of the entire body of believers.

1. The ministerial priesthood has its roots in the apostolic succession and is imbued with sacred power,[2] which consists of the faculty and the

---

[1] Reprinted with permission from *Origins* 39:6 (June 18, 2009)
[2] Cf. Vatican Council II, *Lumen Gentium*, 10, 18, 27, 28; *Presbyterorum Ordinis*, 2, 6; *Catechism of the Catholic Church*, 1538, 1576

responsibility of *acting in the person of Christ, head and shepherd.*[3] "The missionary dimension of the priest is born from his sacramental configuration to Christ the head: This carries with itself as a consequence a happy and total adhesion to that which the tradition of the church has called the *apostolica vivendi forma*. This consists in participating in a spiritually intense 'new life,' in that 'new style of life' which has been inaugurated by the Lord Jesus and has been lived by the apostles themselves. ...

"Certainly a great ecclesial tradition has distinguished the sacramental efficacy from the concrete existential situation of the individual priest, in this way sufficiently safeguarding the legitimate expectations of the faithful. However, this right doctrinal precision takes nothing away from the necessary, indeed the indispensable tension leading toward moral perfection which must find a place in every authentically priestly heart."[4]

Therefore, priests are called to continue the presence of Christ, the one high priest, embodying his way of life and making him visible in the midst of the flock entrusted to their care:[5] This is the true source of strength for every pastoral vocation, which is constituted by the lived coherent testimony of one's consecration, nourished by prayer and penitence.

2. All this is particularly important in understanding the theological reasoning behind priestly *celibacy*, since the will of the church concerning it finds its expression ultimately in that particularly appropriate link which exists between celibacy and priestly ordination whereby the priest is configured to Jesus Christ, head and spouse of the church. The church, being the spouse of Jesus Christ, wishes to be loved in the total and exclusive manner with which Jesus Christ loved her as her head and spouse. Priestly celibacy is therefore the gift of oneself in and with Christ to his church and expresses the service of the priest to the church in and with the Lord.[6]

Indeed, for this reason the church has reaffirmed at the Second Vatican Council and repeatedly in the subsequent pontifical magisterium the "firm will

---

[3] Cf. John Paul II, *Pastores Dabo Vobis*, 15; *Catechism*, 875; Congregation for the Clergy, Pontifical Council for the Laity, Congregation for the Doctrine of the Faith, Congregation for Divine Worship and the Discipline of the Sacraments, Congregation for Bishops, Congregation for the Evangelization of Peoples, Congregation for the Institutes of Consecrated Life and Societies of Apostolic Life, Pontifical Council for the Interpretation of Legislative Texts, "Instruction on Certain Question Regarding the Collaboration of the Nonordained Faithful in the Sacred Ministry of Priests" (Aug. 15, 1997)

[4] Pope Benedict XVI, address to March 16, 2009, clergy congregation general assembly

[5] Cf. *Pastores Dabo Vobis*, 15

[6] Ibid., 29

to maintain the law that demands perpetual and freely chosen celibacy for present and future candidates for priestly ordination in the Latin rite."[7] Priestly celibacy, as indeed apostolic celibacy more generally, is a gift that the church has received and wishes to protect, convinced as she is that this a good for herself and for the world.[8]

To this end Canon 277 of the *Code of Canon Law* states:

> "§1. Clerics are obliged to observe perfect and perpetual continence for the sake of the kingdom of heaven and therefore are bound to celibacy, which is a special gift of God by which sacred ministers can adhere more easily to Christ with an undivided heart and are able to dedicate themselves more freely to the service of God and humanity.
>
> "§2. Clerics are to behave with due prudence toward persons whose company can endanger their obligation to observe continence or give rise to scandal among the faithful.
>
> "§3. The diocesan bishop is competent to establish more specific norms concerning this matter and to pass judgment in particular cases concerning the observance of this obligation."

3. The bishop has, among other things, the duty to remind priests of their obligation to perfect and perpetual continence for the sake of the kingdom of heaven, an obligation freely and willingly assumed by them at the moment of their ordination. Moreover, *the bishop must always be attentive that the priest is faithful in carrying out his proper ministerial duties* (cf. cc. 384, 392). In fact "bishops, as vicars and ambassadors of Christ, govern the particular churches entrusted to them by their counsel, exhortations, example, and even by their authority and sacred power."[9] There exists between them and their priests a *communio sacramentalis* by virtue of the ministerial and hierarchic priesthood, which is a participation in the one priesthood of Christ.[10]

Certainly the bond of subordination between priests and the bishop concerns the area of the exercise of their proper ministry, which they must exercise in hierarchical communion with their own bishop. The relationship which exists between the bishop and his priests cannot, in its canonical aspects, be reduced either to the relationship of hierarchic subordination of public law in the juridical system or to a dependent relationship of an

---

[7] Ibid.; cf. *Presbyterorum Ordinis*, 16; Paul VI, *Sacerdotalis Coelibatus* (June 24, 1967), 14; *Code of Canon Law* c. 277, §1

[8] Cf. Congregation for the Clergy, *Directory for the Ministry and Life of Priests* (Jan. 31, 1994)

[9] *Lumen Gentium*, 27

[10] *Presbyterorum Ordinis*, 7; John Paul II, *Pastores Gregis* (Oct. 16, 2003), 47

employer to an employee.[11] It is not uncommon to find in society those who, misunderstanding the sacramental relationship of the bishop to priest, mistakenly perceive it as the same as that which exists between a director of business and his workforce.

In this type of situation, "since he must protect the unity of the universal church, a bishop is bound to promote the common discipline of the whole church and therefore to urge the observance of all ecclesiastical laws" (c. 392, §1), and he must be vigilant lest abuses insinuate themselves into ecclesiastical discipline (cf. c. 392, §2).

In fact the diocesan bishop must accompany priests with particular concern, ensuring that their rights are protected (cf. c. 384). The vast majority of priests live out their priestly identity daily with serenity and exercise faithfully their proper ministry; but "when situations of scandal arise, especially on the part of the church's ministers, the bishop must act firmly and decisively, justly and serenely. In these lamentable cases the bishop is required to act promptly, according to the established canonical norms, for the spiritual good of the persons involved, for the reparation of scandal, and for the protection and assistance of the victims."[12]

In this context even the penalty ultimately provided for by the bishop "is seen as an instrument of communion that is a means to restore what is lacking in the individual and in the common good when members of the people of God act in an anti-ecclesial manner which is criminal and scandalous."[13]

One must make clear, however, that the diocesan priest, who is not merely the passive executor of commands received from the bishop, enjoys autonomy in making decisions both in his ministry and in his personal and private life. Thus he is personally responsible for his personal actions and for those carried out in the scope of his ministry. As a consequence, a bishop cannot be held juridically responsible for the acts which a diocesan priest carries out in transgression of the canonical norms, universal or particular. This principle is not new and has always been part of the patrimony of the church, means, among other things, that the criminal action of a priest and its penal

---

[11] Cf. Pontifical Council for Legislative Texts, "Explanatory Note: Elements to Establish the Area of Canonical Responsibility of the Diocesan Bishop Toward Clerics Incardinated Within the Diocese and Who Exercise Their Ministry Within It" (Feb. 12, 2004): *Communicationes*, 36 (2004), pp. 33-38. Cf. also Congregation for the Clergy, "Declaration on Some Movements and Associations Forbidden to the Clergy" (March 8, 1982)

[12] Congregation for Bishops, *Directory for the Pastoral Ministry of Bishops* (Feb. 22, 2004), 44.

[13] John Paul II, Feb. 17, 1979, address to the Roman Rota: *Insegnamenti de Giovanni Paolo II* (1979/2), p. 412

consequences as well as any eventual payment of damages is imputable to the priest who has committed the offense and not to the bishop or to the diocese of which the bishop is the legal representative (cf. c. 393).[14]

4. It is reaffirmed that *in exercising his judicial function, the bishop should keep in mind the following general criteria*:

> "(a) Without prejudicing the exercise of justice, the bishop should encourage the faithful to *resolve* their differences *peacefully* and seek to be reconciled at the earliest opportunity, even after the canonical process has begun, thereby avoiding the prolonged animosity to which judicial processes often give rise (cf. c. 1446)
>
> "(b) The bishop should observe and require others to observe the *procedural norms* established for the exercise of judicial power, since he recognizes that these rules are no mere formality, still less an obstacle to be circumvented but are a necessary means for establishing the facts and for administering justice (cf. cc. 135, §3 and 391).
>
> "(c) If he receives notice of behavior which gravely damages the common good of the church, the bishop should investigate with discretion, either by himself or through a delegate, the facts and the imputability of the accused (cf. c. 1717). When he judges that he has assembled sufficient proof of the facts which gave rise to the scandal, he should proceed formally to *correct* or *admonish* the accused (cf. cc. 1339-1340). Yet when this does not suffice to repair the scandal, restore justice and bring about the rehabilitation of the person, the bishop should proceed with the imposition of penalties, which may be applied in either of two ways (cf. cc. 1341 and 1718).
>
> "By means of a regular *penal process* in a case for which canon law requires it, given the gravity of the penalty, or when the bishop judges it more prudent (cf. c. 1721).
>
> "By means of an *extrajudicial decree* in conformity with the procedure established in canon law (cf. c. 1720)."[15]

5. However, one must acknowledge that situations of grave lack of discipline on the part of some clergy have occurred in which the attempts to resolve the problems by the pastoral and canonical means foreseen in the Code of Canon Law are shown to be insufficient or unsuitable to repair scandal, to restore justice or to reform the offender (cf. c. 1341).

---

[14] "Explanatory Note: Elements to Establish the Area of Canonical Responsibility," pp. 33-38

[15] *Directory for the Pastoral Ministry of Bishops*, p. 68

This dicastery, with the intention of promoting the *salus animarum*, the supreme law of the church, and responding to the exigencies often sadly experienced by not a few bishops in their day-to-day-governance, decided that it was opportune to place the aforementioned *special faculties* before the sovereign pontiff for his consideration, and last Jan. 30 the supreme pontiff conceded to this congregation:

> *I. The special faculty to treat and present to the Holy Father, for his approval* in forma specifica *and his decision, cases of dismissal from the clerical state* in poenam *with dispensation from the obligations consequent to ordination, including that of celibacy, of clerics who have attempted marriage, even if only civilly, and who, having been admonished, have not withdrawn from this state, therefore persisting in an irregular and scandalous life (cf. c. 1394, §1); and of clerics guilty of grave sins against the Sixth Commandment (cf. c. 1395, §§1-2).*
>
> *II. The special faculty to intervene in accord with Canon 1399, either by taking direct action in a case or by confirming the decisions of ordinaries, were the competent ordinary so to request, due to the special gravity of the violation of law and the need or urgency to avoid an objective scandal.*
> *This is granted along with the derogation from the prescriptions of Canons 1317, 1319, 1342, §2 and 1349, with respect to the application of perpetual penalties, to be applied to deacons only for grave reasons and to priests for the gravest reasons, always requiring that such cases are presented to the Holy Father for his approval* in forma specifica *and for his decision, and*
>
> *III. The special faculty to handle cases of clerics who having freely abandoned the ministry for a period of more than five consecutive years and who, after careful verification of the facts insofar as this is possible, persist in such freely chosen and illicit absence from the ministry, taking this situation into account, to declare then their dismissal from the clerical state, with dispensation from the obligations consequent to ordination, including that of celibacy.*

Once the necessary conditions are present, if a prelate deems it appropriate to avail himself of the foregoing faculties, he should be aware of the following information and procedures.

6. This congregation has studied the cases of clerics, priests and deacons who:

-Attempt marriage, even civilly and, having been warned, have not withdrawn from this state but instead have persevered in their irregular and scandalous conduct (cf. c. 1394, §1).

-Live in concubinage and commit other grave delicts against the Sixth Commandment of the Decalogue (cf. c. 1395, §§1-2) and who do not demonstrate any sign of mending their ways despite repeated warnings nor show any intention to request the dispensation from the obligations arising from sacred ordination.

Often in such cases the penalty of "suspension" and of irregularity, in the sense of Canon 1044, §1, 3°,[16]have not been demonstrated to be sufficiently effective or suitable to repair the scandal caused, to restore justice and to reform the offender (cf. c. 1341). In fact, only through dismissal from the clerical state, according to the norm of Canon 292, would the cleric also lose the rights pertaining thereto and would no longer be bound by any obligations of that state.

Hence, His Holiness has deigned to concede to the Congregation for the Clergy the special faculties to:

Handle and present to the Holy Father, for his approval *in forma specifica* and decision, cases of dismissal from the clerical state *in poenam* with the consequent dispensation from the obligations consequent to ordination, including that of celibacy, of clerics who have attempted marriage, even if only civilly, and who, having been admonished, have not withdrawn from this state, therefore persisting in an irregular and scandalous life (cf. c. 1394, §1); and of clerics guilty of grave sins against the Sixth Commandment (cf. c. 1395, §§1-2).

---

[16] Cf. also Pontifical Council for Legislative Texts, "Declaration: Concerning the Celebration of Sacraments or Sacramentals by Priests Who Have Attempted Marriage" (May 19, 1997): *Communicationes* 29 (1997), pp. 17-18

Such cases must be instructed by means of a legitimate administrative process, always ensuring the right of defense.

With regard to the administrative procedure (cf. cc. 35-58, 1342, 1720), such cases are to be instructed only by clerics, and it must be ensured that:

1° The accused is notified of the accusations alleged against him and of the relevant proofs, giving him the opportunity to produce a defense unless, having been legitimately cited, he has neglected to make himself available.

2° A careful examination is carried out, with the help of two assessors (cf. c. 1424), of all the proofs and the elements that have been gathered as well as of the defense presented by the accused.

3° A decree is issued, according to the provisions of Canons 1344-1350, if there be no doubts about the delict having been committed, and the criminal action has not become extinct according to the provisions of Canon 1362. The decree, issued according to the norm of Canons 35-38, must contain the reasons motivating it and have expounded therein, even if only in summary fashion, the reasons in law and in fact pertaining to the particular situation.

7. Moreover, it must always be shown that a situation exists in which discipline has been gravely breached by the cleric, and every attempt to resolve the problem through the pastoral and canonical measures already provided in the *Code of Canon Law* have not brought about a positive result, and no end is foreseen to this situation, thus causing grave scandal to the faithful and damaging the common good of the church and her spiritual mission.

In such circumstances, ordinaries have often requested direct action from the Apostolic See or have asked that their decisions be confirmed in order to deal with these matters with greater efficacy and authority, sometimes even seeking the imposition of perpetual sanctions, not excluding dismissal from the clerical state, should the particular circumstances of a case require it.

Therefore, His Holiness has deigned to concede to the Congregation for the Clergy the special faculty to intervene in accord with Canon 1399, either by taking direct action in a case or by confirming the decisions of ordinaries, were the competent ordinary to so request, due to the special gravity of the violation of law and the need or urgency to avoid an objective scandal.

This is granted along with the derogation from the prescriptions of Canons 1317, 1319, 1342, §2 and 1349, with respect to the application of perpetual penalties, to be applied to deacons only for grave reasons and to priests for the gravest reasons, always requiring that such cases are presented to the Holy Father for his approval in forma specifica and his decision.

This provides the special faculty of intervening according to the sense of Canon 1399, either by the dicastery acting directly itself or by confirming the decisions of ordinaries, whenever the competent ordinary should request this, in order to apply a just penalty or penance for an external violation of divine or canon law. In truly exceptional and urgent cases, when the offender has no intention to amend his ways, sometimes even perpetual penalties may be imposed.

Such cases must be instructed by means of a legitimate administrative process, always ensuring the right of defense.

8. This congregation has experience of cases of priests and deacons who have abandoned ministry for a prolonged and continuous time. In these cases, after verifying the circumstances insofar as possible, the persistence of such an illicit and voluntary absence from ministry is ascertained, it was decided that the intervention of the Holy See would guarantee order in the ecclesiastical society and would preserve the faithful from falling into *error communis* (cf. c. 144) regarding the validity of the sacraments.

Therefore His Holiness has deigned to concede to the Congregation for the Clergy the special faculty to:

Handle the cases of clerics who have abandoned the ministry by personal choice for a period of more than five consecutive years and, after careful verification of the facts insofar as this is possible, persist in such voluntary and illicit absence, the dicastery, taking this objective situation into account, may declare the dismissal from the clerical state, with dispensation from the obligations consequent to ordination, including that of celibacy, for the cleric involved.

Such cases, even those pre-existing the granting of this faculty, must be instructed according to the following procedure:

Article 1. The ordinary of incardination may request a rescript of the Apostolic See by which dismissal from the clerical state is declared, along with the related dispensations from the obligations consequent to ordination, including that of celibacy, for a cleric who has abandoned ministry for a period of longer than five consecutive years and who after careful verification of the facts, insofar as possible, persists in the voluntary and illicit absence from ministry.

Article 2, §1. The competent ordinary is that of the incardination of the cleric.

§2. The competent ordinary can entrust the instruction of such procedures either in a stable manner or on a case-by-case basis to a suitable priest from his own or another diocese.

§3. In this procedure the promoter of justice, who has a duty to protect the public good, must always be involved.

Article 3. The declaration mentioned in Article 1 can be obtained only after the competent ordinary, having completed the relevant investigation, has reached moral certainty regarding the irreversible abandonment from ministry on the part of the cleric, from either the declaration of the cleric himself and/or from the depositions of witnesses, from well-founded public knowledge or other indications.

Article 4. The notification of any of the acts must be made through the postal service or by other secure means.

Article 5. The instructor, having completed the instruction, should transmit all of the acts to the competent ordinary with his appropriate summary, expounding his *votum* according to the objective facts of the situation.

Article 6. The competent ordinary should transmit to the Apostolic See all of the acts together with his own *votum* and the observations of the promoter of justice.

Article 7. If in the judgment of the Apostolic See supplementary instruction is required, that will be indicated to the competent ordinary, with directions as to how to complete the "acts."

Article 8. The rescript of dismissal from the clerical state, with the related dispensation from the obligations attendant upon holy orders, including that of celibacy, is transmitted from the Holy See to the competent ordinary, who will provide for making it known in an appropriate fashion.

9. After the dismissal from the clerical state, in exceptional cases, a cleric who might wish to seek rehabilitation must present that request to the Apostolic See through a benevolent bishop.

The sincere desire of this congregation is that each ordinary may, in a truly paternal fashion and in a spirit of pastoral charity, undertake to ensure that his most valued collaborators know how to live ecclesiastical discipline as "discipleship," with profound interior motivations, remembering that the daily exertion of "doing" is of little value if there is not the "being in Christ" as an authentic disciple.

(signed) Cardinal Cláudio Hummes
Prefect

(signed)Archbishop Mauro Piacenza
Secretary

CANONS 1317; 1342, §2; 1349; 1399

SPECIAL FACULTIES FOR CONGREGATION FOR EVANGELIZATION OF PEOPLES
ADMINISTRATIVE PROCEDURE FOR THE LAICIZATION OF PRIESTS, DEACONS AND MEMBERS OF INSTITUTES OF CONSECRATED LIFE AND SOCIETIES OF APOSTOLIC LIFE FOR *MISSIO AD GENTES*

On December 19, 2009 Pope Benedict XVI granted the Congregation for the Evangelization of Peoples special faculties for resolving cases involving requests for dispensation from clerical obligations for priests and deacons of mission dioceses and members of Societies of Apostolic Life for missio ad gentes *that depend on the Congregation. The faculties enable the Congregation to address promptly serious cases of scandalous behavior by clerics that call for an urgent decision. The faculties provide additional means not available in the Code of Canon Law to resolve grave violations of clerical celibacy or situations where clerics have abandoned their ministry for an extended period of time. The text of the communication sent to Major Superiors of Societies of Apostolic Life* for missio ad gentes *follows:*

Letter to Superiors General, Missionary Societies of Apostolic Life (dependent on the Congregation for the Evangelization of Peoples)

Congregation for the Evangelization of Peoples
March 31, 2009
Prot. N. 0579/09

Dear and Very Rev. Fr. Superior General,

I write to inform you that during the Audience granted me on December 19, 2008, the Holy Father Pope Benedict XVI, taking into account the particular circumstances of Mission territories, granted to the Congregation for the Evangelization of Peoples some Special Faculties, without prejudice, however, to the ordinary competencies of other Dicasteries of the Holy See. These faculties enable this Congregation to deal promptly with serious cases of scandal – certainly with due respect to the natural right of the accused persons to defend themselves – caused by indiscipline on the part of clerics, that require an urgent decision for avoiding the continuation of the scandal and greater spiritual damage to the Church and to the persons concerned.

The Holy Father further decided that the Societies of Apostolic Life for *missio ad gentes*, that depend on this Congregation, should come under the purview of the present Special Faculties, which authorize this Dicastery:

1. To proceed administratively and bring to the approval *in forma specifica* and decision of the Holy Father cases regarding the dismissal in *peonam* from the clerical status of those clerics who are found guilty of the offenses defined in ca. 1395, §§ 1&2 (concubinage and other serious sexual scandals), without prejudice to the exclusive competence of the Congregation for the Doctrine of the Faith regarding cases of pedophilia.
   -The same penalty is also applied to a cleric who is guilty of attempted marriage and, though duly admonished by the competent Ordinary, refuses to mend his ways and continues in his irregular and scandalous life (cf. can. 1394, §1).
   -The same penalty could also be applied to a deacon who has caused scandal in the moral field and is therefore judged by the competent Superior not fit to be promoted to the Order of priesthood, but does not intend to ask for the pontifical dispensation from the obligations arising from the diaconate Ordination.
2. To study, following the existing procedure, and bring directly to the decision of the Holy Father requests for dispensation from clerical obligations, presented by members of the Societies of Apostolic Life for *missio ad gentes* that depend on this Dicastery.
3. To act in accordance with the provisions of can. 1399, either directly or confirming the decisions of competent Superiors, when they ask for it, in particularly serious cases of violation of law, when there is an urgent need to avoid an objective scandal.
4. The Holy Father has, moreover, graciously granted the derogation from the provisions of cann. 1317, 1342, § 2, and 1349, that deal with the application of perpetual sanctions, to be inflicted on deacons for serious reasons and on priests for very serious reasons, always bringing individual cases directly to the Holy Father for his approval *in forma specifica* and decision.

Eventual requests for applying the above mentioned Special Faculties should be instructed according to the enclosed indications. The observance of this procedure and the completeness of the documentation are necessary for avoiding undue delays in studying and deciding the cases presented.

While communicating the above for your information, I take this opportunity to extend to you kind regards and prayerful best wishes, and I remain,

Yours devotedly in *Corde Mariae*,

(signed) Ivan Cardinal Dias
Prefect

(signed) Most Rev. Archbishop Robert Sarah
Secretary

Enclosures

Congregation for the Evangelization of Peoples
March 31, 2009
Prot. N. 0579/09

Request for Dispensation from Clerical Obligations Presented by Priests and Deacons

During the Audience granted to the Cardinal Prefect on 19 December 2009, the Holy Father Pope Benedict XVI graciously granted to the Congregation for the Evangelization of Peoples the Special Faculty to study the requests for dispensation from clerical obligations presented by priests and deacons of mission dioceses and members of Societies of Apostolic Life for the *missio ad gentes* that depend on the same Mission Dicastery, as well as for members of Institutes of Consecrated Life and Societies of Apostolic Life of diocesan right, who have their principal houses in mission territories, and to bring these cases directly to the supreme decision of the Holy Father.

It is necessary, first of all, to remember that when a cleric shows signs of weakness and vocational crisis, or of difficulties in his ministry, the Ordinary of the place or the Superior of the Institute should show him every paternal understanding and offer him the help and necessary spiritual and professional assistance, in order to support and encourage him to overcome the crisis and difficulties.

If the cleric, after a serious process of mature reflection, prayer and discernment, decides to definitively leave the clerical state and ask for the pontifical dispensation from all clerical obligations, the Ordinary of the place or the competent Superior should instruct the case and prepare a dossier that should contain the following documents:

1. A letter of the priest or deacon in question, written in all sincerity and addressed to the Holy Father, in which he explains the reasons of his vocational crisis and eventual defection from the priesthood; also describing the reasons for considering his decision to seek the pontifical dispensation irreversible.
   The above petition that the interested cleric should personally sign, should ask for both the dispensation from all his clerical obligations as well as the reduction to the lay state.
2. A detailed *curriculum vitae* of the petitioner, indicating the various stages and the important dates in his life, as well as in his formation and clerical ministry.
3. A document in which the Ordinary summarizes all the attempts he has made to dissuade the petitioner from presenting the request for dispensation, and all the assistance given him to help overcome his crisis and to motivate him to return to the priestly life and ministry. For this purpose, the petitioner's Ordinary, either personally or through a priest delegate, may collect any useful information regarding the cleric in question, possibly interrogating the same cleric and some other witnesses who know him well, as, for example, a formator, a seminary companion or brother-priest, or also a co-worker.
   A dossier should also contain the "*votum*" of the Ordinary of the place (or of the Superior General, in the case of a member of an institute) regarding the merit of the case, as well as the absence of scandal in the place where the petitioner is actually living. Moreover, it is advisable that this *votum* be corroborated by the College of consultors of the diocese of incardination of the petitioner or by the General Council of the institute to which he belongs.
4. A document which proves that the petitioner has been suspended from exercising the sacred ministry from the moment his petition for dispensation has been presented to and accepted by the competent Ordinary/Superior.

5. An authenticated copy of the document regarding the eventual attempted marriage of the petitioner and the application or declaration of canonical sanctions against him.
6. Documents written in the vernacular language should be translated into a European language, preferably Italian, English or French, and the manuscripts and other legal documents should be typewritten.
7. The complete dossier, prepared in an orderly manner and put together with a progressive page numbering and a table of contents, should be sent to the Congregation for the Evangelization of Peoples, through the Apostolic Nuncio in the country, who is required to give his own opinion on the case.

(signed) Ivan Cardinal Dias
Prefect

(signed) Most Rev. Archbishop Robert Sarah
Secretary

Canon 1382

DECREE LIFTING EXCOMMUNICATION LATAE SENTENTIAE OF THE BISHOPS OF THE SOCIETY OF ST. PIUS X

Pope Benedict XVI remitted the excommunications of four bishops ordained against papal orders in 1988 by the late French Archbishop Marcel Lefebvre. The decree was released January 24, 2009 by the Vatican Congregation for Bishops and signed by Cardinal Giovanni Battista Re, prefect of the congregation that declared the excommunications in July 1988. The decree states that Pope Benedict, "in his paternal compassion for the spiritual discomfort expressed by the parties concerned," hopes that this action will "consolidate reciprocal relations of trust" and "intensify and stabilize" relations between the Holy See and the Society of St. Pius X. It also says the hope is that the move will lead to the "prompt attainment of full communion with the church by the entire Fraternity of St. Pius X." The decree was released in Italian; a Vatican Information Service translation follows:

Congregation for Bishops
January 21, 2009

Decree

In a letter of 15 December 2008 addressed to Cardinal Dario Castrillon Hoyos, President of the Pontifical Commission "Ecclesia Dei," Mons. Bernard Fellay writing also in the name of the other three Bishops consecrated on 30 June 1988 requested once again the removal of the excommunication *latae sententiae* formally declared by a Decree of the Prefect of this Congregation for Bishops on 1 July 1988.

In his letter, Mons. Fellay stated, among other things, that "we continue firmly resolute in our desire to remain Catholics and to put all our strength at the service of the Church of our Lord Jesus Christ, which is the Roman Catholic Church. We accept her teachings in a filial spirit. We firmly believe in the primacy of Peter and in his prerogatives, and for this reason the current situation causes us much suffering."

His Holiness Benedict XVI in his paternal concern for the spiritual distress which the parties concerned have voiced as a result of the excommunication, and trusting in their commitment, expressed in the aforementioned letter, to spare no effort in exploring as yet unresolved questions through requisite discussions with the authorities of the Holy See in order to reach a prompt, full and satisfactory solution to the original problem has decided to reconsider to canonical situation of Bishops Bernard Fellay, Bernard Tissier de Mallerais, Richard Williamson and Alfonso de Galarreta, resulting from their episcopal consecration.

This act signifies a desire to strengthen reciprocal relations of trust, and to deepen and stabilize the relationship of the Society of St. Pius X with this Apostolic See. This gift of peace, coming at the end of the Christmas celebrations, is also meant to be a sign which promotes the Universal Church's unity in charity, and removes the scandal of division.

It is hoped that this step will be followed by the prompt attainment of full communion with the Church on the part of the whole Society of St. Pius X, which will thus bear witness to its genuine fidelity and genuine recognition of the Magisterium and authority of the Pope by the proof of visible unity.

On the basis of the powers expressly granted to me by the Holy Father Benedict XVI, by virtue of the present Decree I remit the penalty of excommunication *latae sententiae* incurred by Bishops Bernard Fellay, Bernard Tissier de Mallerais, Richard Williamson and Alfonso de Galarreta, and declared by this Congregation on 1 July 1988. At the same time I declare that, as of today's date, the Decree issued at that time no longer has juridical effect.

(signed) Cardinal Giovanni Battista Re
Prefect

Pastor Bonus n. 108, §1

Apostolic Visitation of Women Religious in the United States

The Congregation for Institutes of Consecrated Life and Societies of Apostolic Life (CICLSAL) has the authority to intervene in those matters reserved to the Holy See regarding consecrated life (cf. Pastor Bonus, *108, §1). Cardinal Franc Rode, Prefect of the Congregation, with the faculties granted to him by His Holiness Pope Benedict XVI in an audience on November 17, 2008, issued a decree naming Mother Mary Clare Millea, superior general of the Apostles of the Sacred Heart of Jesus, as Apostolic Visitator* ad inquirendum et referendum *to look into the quality of the life of women religious in the United States. Upon completion of this apostolic visitation, Mother Mary Clare Millea will forward to the CICLSAL a detailed report. The text of the Prefect's decree follows:*

Congregation for Institutes of Consecrated Life and Societies of Apostolic Life
December 22, 2008
Prot. N. 16805/2008

Decree

The Congregation for Institutes of Consecrated Life and Societies of Apostolic Life has the task of intervening in all that is reserved to the Holy See regarding consecrated life (cf. Pastor Bonus n. 108, §1). In order to look into the quality of the life of religious women in the United States, the Prefect of this Dicastery, with the faculties granted to him by His Holiness Pope Benedict XVI, in an audience on November 17, 2008, has decided to nominate, and with the present decree nominates,

> Reverend Mother Mary Clare MILLEA,
> Superior General of the Apostles of the Sacred Heart of Jesus
>
> Apostolic Visitator *ad inquirendum et referendum* of the General Houses, Provincial Houses and Centers of Initial Formation, of the principal Religious Institutes of Women in the United States of America.

Upon completion of this Apostolic Visitation, the Apostolic Visitator will also seek information from those Diocesan Bishops in whose Dioceses the abovementioned General Houses, Provincial Houses and Centers of Initial Formation are located.

All things to the contrary notwithstanding.

(signed) Cardinal Franc Rodé, CM
Prefect

(signed) Archbishop Gianfranco A. Gardin, OFM Conv.
Archbishop Secretary

ADVISORY OPINIONS

INTRODUCTORY NOTE

The following opinions were developed in response to inquiries received by the Editor of CLSA Advisory Opinions or assembled by the Editor from among those submitted to the Society for publication. The opinions carry only the weight of the persons named at the end of each opinion. They do not represent the opinion of the diocese or institution to which the author is affiliated nor of the Canon Law Society of America. Advisory opinions are not authentic interpretations of the law, but reflect the scholarly and practical insights of the contributors.

The opinions are arranged according to the canons of the Code of Canon Law and the Code of Canons of the Eastern Churches. The original questions have been abbreviated or summarized, and the opinions lightly edited to protect the anonymity of the inquirer or to conform to the style of Canon Law Society of America publications.

The Editor expresses profound gratitude to the canonists who participated in this year's publication. The continued success of this annual project is a result of their willingness to share their time and talent in service to this important work.

The Canon Law Society of America is interested in receiving opinions that members have formulated in response to specific inquiries, and inquiries in need of responses. It also welcomes the participation of members who wish to be involved in this annual project by offering to render opinions to inquiries received by the Committee.

Inquiries or contributions to CLSA Advisory Opinions may be directed to the Office of the Executive Coordinator at:

Canon Law Society of America
Office of the Executive Coordinator
The Hecker Center, Suite 111
3025 Fourth Street, N.E.
Washington, DC 20017-1102
(202) 832-2350

Siobhan M. Verbeek, J.C.L., *Editor*

CANON 2

ADOPTING PRE-CONCILIAR LITURGICAL PRACTICES IN THE CELEBRATION OF THE ORDINARY FORM OF THE MASS

A priest of our diocese recently introduced several changes into the celebration of the Mass, most of which were commonplace before the liturgical reforms following the Second Vatican Council. These changes include: (1) placing six large candlesticks and a crucifix on the altar; (2) wearing a biretta, maniple, and the so-called "fiddleback" chasuble; and (3) celebrating one Sunday Mass ad orientem, *that is, facing the apse of the Church. He cites the writings and practices of Pope Benedict XVI to justify the reintroduction of these liturgical practices. Are these permitted in the celebration of the ordinary form of the Mass?*

OPINION

The earlier writings of Cardinal Joseph Ratzinger, along with the promulgation of the Apostolic Letter *motu proprio*, *Summorum Pontificum*, by Pope Benedict XVI, have reinvigorated interest in pre-conciliar liturgical forms.[1] The questions above are illustrative of the confusion many experience, especially in determining which laws are applicable to the ordinary and extraordinary forms of the one Roman rite. Resolution of these matters can be difficult and appear somewhat arbitrary, inasmuch as certain practices are permitted for one form of the Roman rite, but not the other. The following resolution is offered, aware that an authoritative response or clarification may be offered at any time by the Holy See.

1 – Candles and Crucifix

---

[1] See, for example, Cardinal Joseph Ratzinger, *The Feast of Faith: Approaches to a Theology of the Liturgy*, trans. Graham Harrison (San Francisco: Ignatius Press, 1986); Cardinal Joseph Ratzinger, *The Spirit of the Liturgy*, trans. John Saward (San Francisco: Ignatius Press, 2000); and Pope Benedict XVI, Apostolic Letter *motu proprio*, *Summorum Pontificum*, "On the Use of Pre-conciliar Liturgical Forms," July 7, 2007, *Acta Apostolicae Sedis* 99 (2007) 777-781; English translation in *Origins* 37 (2007-2008) 129-132.

The latest *General Instruction of the Roman Missal* (*GIRM*)[2] provides a rather clear directive concerning the use of candles at Mass and can be summarized as follows: (1) Candles are required at every liturgical service out of reverence and on account of the festiveness of the celebration; (2) candles are to be appropriately placed either on or around the altar; (3) the placement of the candles is to be suited to the design of the altar and the sanctuary; and (4) candles are not to interfere with the faithful's clear view of what takes place at the altar or what is placed on it (no. 307). The *GIRM* specifies that at least two candles are to be used in any celebration, but four or even six candles can be used, especially for Sunday Mass or a holy day of obligation. If a diocesan bishop celebrates, then seven candles are to be used. Furthermore, on or close to the altar, there is to be a cross with a figure of Christ crucified (no. 117). The arrangement of seven candles and a crucifix upon the altar has been frequently employed at Masses celebrated by Pope Benedict XVI, most notably since the appointment of Msgr. Guido Marini as Papal Master of Ceremonies. So long as the placement of the candles and crucifix are suited to the design of the altar and the sanctuary and do not obstruct the view of the faithful, no reasonable objections can be raised to the arrangement described above.

2 – Liturgical Vestments

The use of the maniple—an ornamental vestment worn on the left arm during Mass—was already made optional in 1967 by means of the instruction Tres abhinc annos.3 The biretta is a quadrangular head covering with three peaks and frequently surmounted with a pompon. Although employed at Mass prior to the revised Missale Romanum, the biretta has never been listed among sacred vestments.4 Summorum Pontificum has permitted wider use of the Missal of Blessed John XXIII, including the observance of its rubrics which

---

[2] *Missale Romanum, Ex editione typica tertia*, April 20, 2000 (Vatican City: Libreria Editrice Vaticana, 2000). An English translation of the *Institutio Generalis Missalis Romani*, which prefaces the *Missale Romanum*, can be found in *General Instruction of the Roman Missal*, Liturgy Documentary Series 2 (United States Conference of Catholic Bishops: Washington, DC, 2003).

[3] Congregation for Sacred Rites, Instruction, *Tres abhinc annos*, May 4, 1967, no. 25, *Acta Apostolicae Sedis* 59 (1967) 442-448. It would be incorrect to presume that use of the maniple remains optional on the basis of this document. *Tres abhinc annos* introduced a number of provisional adaptations to the 1962 Roman Missal, much like the Instruction *Inter oecumenici* three years earlier. See *Acta Apostolicae Sedis* 56 (1964) 877-900. These instructions were intended for application with the 1962 Roman Missal, not the revised *Missale Romanum* of 1970.

[4] See Henry J. McCloud, *Clerical Dress and Insignia of the Roman Catholic Church* (Milwaukee: Bruce Publishing Co., 1948), 61.

prescribe, among other things, the use of the maniple and biretta.[5] The revised *Missale Romanum* of Paul VI and its accompanying *institutio generalis*, conversely, make no mention of either the maniple or biretta. The recent *GIRM* clearly specifies that the vestment proper to a priest celebrant at Mass is the chasuble, worn over the alb and stole.[6]

Optional use of the maniple or biretta should not be inferred on the basis that the GIRM or the rubrics of the *Missale Romanum* do not explicitly exclude their use. A similar question concerning proper methods for incensation was addressed to the Congregation for Divine Worship, which responded as follows:

> It must never be forgotten that the *Missal* of Pope Paul VI has, since 1970, supplanted the one called improperly 'the *Missal* of St. Pius V,' and completely so, in both text and rubrics. When the rubrics of the *Missal* of Paul VI say nothing or say little on particulars in some places, it is not to be inferred that the former rite should be observed. Therefore, the multiple and complex gestures for incensation as prescribed in the former *Missal* ... are not to be resumed.[7]

Similarly, when asked about the appropriate gestures to accompany the Confiteor, *Agnus Dei*, and *Domine, non sum dignus*, the Congregation responded as follows:

> [W]hen the rubrics of the *Missal* of Paul VI say nothing, it is not to be thereby inferred that the former rubrics must be followed. The reformed *Missal* does not supplement but supplants the old *Missal*. The old *Missal* at the *Agnus Dei* had the directive 'striking his breast three times' and the same for the *Domine, non sum dignus*. But because the new *Missal* says nothing on this point (*Ordo*

---

[5] See, for example, the *Ritus servandus in celebratione Missae*, Tit. II, nos. 1, 2, 5; Tit. XII, nos. 6-7.

[6] *General Instruction of the Roman Missal*, no. 337; see also no. 119a. The biretta is a commonly prescribed part of "choir dress" for cardinals, bishops, and other prelates. See Secretariat of State, Instruction, *Ut sive sollicite*, March 31, 1969, *Acta Apostolicae Sedis* 61 (1969) 334-340; English translation in *Canon Law Digest* 7:137-143; Sacred Congregation for the Clergy, Circular Letter, *Per Instructionem*, October 30, 1970, *Acta Apostolicae Sedis* 63 (1970) 314-315; English translation in *Canon Law Digest* 7:382-383. The *Ceremonial of Bishops*, no. 66, provides the following norm: "Presbyters who take part in a liturgical service but not as concelebrants are to wear choir dress if they are prelates or canons, cassock and surplice if they are not." See *Caeremoniale Episcoporum*, editio typica, September 14, 1984 (Vatican City: Typis Polyglottis Vaticanis, 1984), 28. Conspicuously absent is mention of the use of the biretta by ordinary priests.

[7] Congregation for Divine Worship, *Responsum ad dubium*, in *Notitiae* 14 (1978) 301-302, no. 2; English translation in International Commission on English in the Liturgy, *Documents on the Liturgy 1963-1979: Conciliar, Papal, and Curial Texts* (Collegeville, MN: The Liturgical Press, 1982), 481, footnote R11.

Missae, nn. 131 and 133), there is no reason for requiring any gesture to be added to these invocations.[8]

Some may object that the line of argumentation employed here by the Congregation for Divine Worship—nearly thirty years ago—has been superseded by *Summorum Pontificum*. In his letter to bishops accompanying the Apostolic Letter, Pope Benedict XVI suggests that the ordinary and extraordinary forms of the Roman rite can be "mutually enriching."[9] Although it is not entirely clear how this will be achieved, it is not inconceivable that the use of certain vestments, such as the maniple, and the return of certain practices may find renewed expression in the liturgy. Before this can occur, however, a change in law or a clarification from the Holy See is required. Until such a time, it does not appear that the use of the maniple or biretta by priests celebrating the ordinary form of the Mass is permitted.[10] This is supported not only by responses of the Congregation for Divine Worship, but by a general norm of law which states that a later law abrogates or derogates from an earlier law if it states so expressly, is directly contrary to it, or completely reorders the entire matter of the earlier law (c. 20). With the promulgation of the revised *Ordo Missae* and *GIRM*, the *Rubricae Generales*, the *Ritus Servandus in Celebratione Missae*, and the *De Defectibus in Celebratione Missae* of the 1962 *Missale Romanum* were explicitly abrogated.[11]

The chasuble—the outermost vestment proper to a priest at Mass—has taken on various shapes and sizes throughout history. The "fiddleback" or "Roman" style chasuble was predominant before the liturgical reforms of the

---

[8] Congregation for Divine Worship, *Responsum ad dubium*, in *Notitiae* 14 (1978) 535, no. 10; English translation in International Commission on English in the Liturgy, *Documents on the Liturgy 1963-1979: Conciliar, Papal, and Curial Texts* (Collegeville, MN: The Liturgical Press, 1982), 491, footnote R22. This line of argumentation was extended by the United States Conference of Catholic Bishops' Committee on the Liturgy to questions concerning use of the *manatergium* in the ordination of a priest. It responded as follows: "By extension, it may be safely stated that no rite described in a pre-conciliar liturgical book may be introduced into a post-conciliar rite. The suppression of the pre-conciliar rite includes the suppression of all texts and rubrics included in that rite." See *BCL Newsletter*, August 2002, at http://www.usccb.org/liturgy/innews/082002.shtml [accessed June 2009].

[9] Pope Benedict XVI, Letter to Bishops Accompanying the Apostolic Letter *Summorum Pontificum*, July 7, 2007, *Acta Apostolicae Sedis* 99 (2007) 795-799; English translation in *Origins* 37 (2007-2008) 132-134.

[10] For an alternate opinion concerning use of the biretta, see James-Charles Noonan, Jr., *The Church Visible: The Ceremonial Life and Protocol of the Roman Catholic Church* (New York: Viking Penguin, 1996), 299-304.

[11] Sacred Congregation of Rites, Decree, *Ordine Missae*, April 6, 1969, in *Notitiae* 5 (1969) 147; English translation in *Canon Law Digest* 7:620-621.

Second Vatican Council. Even before the Council, however, requests for use of the more ample "Gothic" form of the chasuble resulted in a noteworthy concession by the Congregation for Sacred Rites, which had hitherto restricted its use.[12] There is presently no restriction on the use of the so-called "fiddleback" chasuble. Instead, the *GIRM* identifies some basic principles for the design and construction of liturgical vestments, permitting, where necessary, local adaptations by conferences of bishops (see *GIRM*, nos. 335-347). The beauty and nobility of each vestment should derive from the material and design used, rather than "overly lavish ornamentation" (*GIRM*, no. 344).

3 – Celebration *Ad Orientem*

The *GIRM* (no. 299) provides a rather clear directive on the placement of the altar and the direction one is to face when celebrating Mass:

> The altar should be built apart from the wall, in such a way that it is possible to walk around it easily and that Mass can be celebrated at it facing the people, which is desirable whenever possible. The altar should, moreover, be so placed as to be truly the center toward which the attention of the whole congregation of the faithful naturally turns. The altar is to be fixed and is dedicated.

Asked whether *GIRM*, no. 299 excluded the position *ad orientem* during the Eucharistic liturgy, the Congregation for Divine Worship and the Discipline of the Sacraments replied "*Negative et ad mentem*":

> Above all one must recall that the word *expedient* does not constitute an obligatory norm, but a suggestion which refers either to the construction of the altar *separate from the wall*, or to celebration facing the people. The phrase *where possible* refers to different elements, such as, for example, the layout of the place, the availability of space, the existence of a previous altar of artistic value, the sensibility of the community which participates in the celebrations in the Church in question, etc. One confirms that the position facing the assembly seems more appropriate in as much as

---

[12] Sacred Congregation of Rites, Declaration, "Gothic" Vestments, August 20 1957, *Acta Apostolicae Sedis* 49 (1957) 762; English translation in *Canon Law Digest* 4:262. An earlier response of the same Congregation, to which this refers, had restricted the use of "Gothic" style vestments without permission from the Holy See. See Sacred Congregation of Rites, Reply, "Gothic" Vestments, December 9, 1925, *Acta Apostolicae Sedis* 18 (1926) 58; English translation in *Canon Law Digest* 1:374.

it renders communication easier (see Editorial in *Notitiae* 29 [1993], 245-249), but without excluding the alternative possibility.[13]

The same Congregation, however, confirmed that it is "incorrect and indeed quite unacceptable" to affirm that the celebration of Mass *ad orientem* "is a theologically preferable or more orthodox choice for a priest who wishes to be true to the Church's authentic tradition."[14]

Pope Benedict XVI has celebrated Mass *ad orientem* on a few occasions. These celebrations occurred in the Sistine Chapel where the altar is fixed to the wall. Although not presented as the ideal, the law does not exclude the celebration of Mass *ad orientem* in these and similar circumstances.

It is one thing to celebrate *ad orientem* on altars which display historic or artistic merit, or in sanctuaries lacking in space for the addition of a freestanding altar; it is quite another to remove a freestanding altar in favor of constructing an altar fixed to the wall, seemingly to accommodate the preferences of the priest-celebrant. To do this would be a violation of the law. The Rite of Dedication of a Church and an Altar, in Chapter IV, no. 8, says: "The altar should be freestanding so that the priest can easily walk around it and celebrate Mass facing the people."[15] Diocesan bishops, as "the principal dispensers of the mysteries of God, and the directors, promoters, and guardians of the entire liturgical life in the church entrusted to them," should attend to this matter expeditiously (c. 835, §1). Bishops can be assisted in this task by the diocesan liturgical commission and by guidelines issued for the construction and renovation of churches by the appropriate conference of bishops.

Nevertheless, should a priest, attentive to the needs and sensibilities of the faithful, choose to celebrate Mass *ad orientem* for legitimate reasons, he does so fully in accordance with the law. Since the priest in question is celebrating only one Sunday Mass *ad orientem*, the faithful are free to choose which Mass

---

[13] Congregation for Divine Worship and the Discipline of the Sacraments, Reply Concerning the Celebration of Mass *ad orientem*, September 25, 2000, in *Communicationes* 32 (2000) 171-173; English translation in *Canon Law Society of Great Britain & Ireland Newsletter*, no. 126 (June 2001), 47.

[14] Congregation for Divine Worship and the Discipline of the Sacraments, Reply Concerning the Position of the Priest Celebrant at Mass, in *Roman Replies and CLSA Advisory Opinions 2000*, eds. F. Stephen Pedone and James I. Donlon (Washington, DC: Canon Law Society of America, 2000), 33-35.

[15] *Rite of Dedication of a Church and an Altar*, May, 29 1977, in International Commission on English in the Liturgy, *Documents on the Liturgy 1963-1979: Conciliar, Papal, and Curial Texts* (Collegeville, MN: The Liturgical Press, 1982), 1380, no. 4405.

they wish to attend, much like the choice between children's Masses or Masses celebrated with a traditional choir. This appears to be a satisfactory solution, inasmuch as it attempts to accommodate the needs and sensibilities of the parish community.

Chad J. Glendinning, J.C.L.

CANON 127, §1

USING ELECTRONIC MEANS OF COMMUNICATION FOR CONSULTATION

Large distances separate the members of a group with whom a superior is required to consult, thereby making the convocation of a meeting of the group–where everyone is physically present–very difficult. On other occasions, while a quorum of the members can be physically present, not everyone can be physically present. Could electronic means of communication be used to allow those who cannot be physically present to participate and be present through these means, assuming of course that the electronic means allow the members to hear and interact with one another, and all documents and information are available to everyone participating?

OPINION

Since the promulgation and coming into force of the 1983 *Code of Canon Law*, electronic means of communication that allow members of a group to be present for a meeting have expanded, advanced in quality, and become more readily accessible. In addition to telephone conferencing, we now have audio-visual conferencing, internet conferencing, and other means of conferencing that allow not just audio participation but the sharing of documents and other information. These electronic means allow those who are not physically present to be electronically present and to participate as fully in the meeting as those who are physically present. Whether electronic means, therefore, can be used when a superior needs to consult a group is an interesting question, and the answer depends on whether counsel or consent is being sought.

The law governing consultation is found in canon 127, §1[1], which states:

> When it is established by law that in order to place acts a superior needs the consent or counsel of some college or group of persons, the college or group of persons must be convoked according to the norms of can. 166 unless, when it concerns seeking counsel only, particular or proper law provides otherwise. For such acts to be valid, however, it is required that the consent of an absolute majority of those present is obtained or that the counsel of all is sought.

[1] Canon 934, §1 of the Code of Canons of the Eastern Churches is similar.

Canon 166 concerns the giving of proper notice of the time and place of the meeting, which could be given not just when members were expected to be physically present, but also when members would be allowed to be present and participate through electronic means.

In regards to counsel, various methods of obtaining it can be provided. While the preference is to gather together the members of the group and hear them, canon 127, §1 allows for particular or proper law to provide for other methods of obtaining counsel, rather than gathering the members together physically. Particular or proper law could, therefore, allow for all the members of the group to be contacted individually for their counsel without ever gathering the group, including individual telephone calls, letters or facsimiles.[2] Using electronic means for members to be present at a meeting and participate is less extreme than not gathering the group, because electronic means allow the members of the group to interact and engage in discussion which can enhance or change the counsel given. Commentators seem to be in agreement that electronic means can be used when gathering a group to provide counsel, provided the statutes so allow it.[3]

In regards to consent, canon 127, §1 clearly requires that the group be gathered in order to validly give consent. Unlike for counsel, there is no provision for particular or proper law to allow for other methods of obtaining consent. Commentators are split on whether members of the group must be physically present for the group to give consent[4] or whether some or all of the members can be present through electronic means.[5]

---

[2] See Richard A. Hill, S.J., "Juridic Acts," in The Code of Canon Law: A Text and Commentary, eds. James A Coriden, Thomas J. Green, and Donald E. Heintschel (New York, NY: Paulist Press, 1985), 91; Augustine Mendonça, "The Legitimate Method for Contacting the College of Consultors," in CLSA Advisory Opinions 2001-2005, ed. Arthur J. Espalage, O.F.M. (Alexandria, VA: Canon Law Society of America, 2006), 58-64; Helmuth Pree, "On Juridic Acts and Liability in Canon Law: Part Two," The Jurist 58 (1998) 488-489; James H. Provost, "Presbyteral Councils and Colleges of Consultors: Current Law and Some Diocesan Statutes," CLSA Proceedings 49 (1987) 210; Michael Thériault, Commentary on Canon 127, in Exegetical Commentary on the Code of Canon Law, eds. Ángel Marzoa, Jorge Miras, and Rafael Rodríguez-Ocaña (Montréal: Wilson & Lafleur, 2004), I:810; Myriam Wijlens, "Juridic Acts, " in New Commentary on the Code of Canon Law, eds. John P. Beal, James A. Coriden, and Thomas J. Green (New York, NY: Paulist Press, 2000), 181; William H. Woestman, O.M.I., "Advice and Consent of the College of Consultors," in CLSA Advisory Opinions 1994-2000, ed. Arthur J. Espelage, O.F.M. (Washington, DC: Canon Law Society of America, 2002), 19-21.

[3] Ibid.

[4] See James H. Provost, "Manner of Superior Seeking Council's Consent," in CLSA Advisory Opinions 1994-2000, ed. Arthur J. Espelage, O.F.M. (Washington, DC: Canon Law Society of America, 2002), 18-19; James H. Provost, "Presbyteral Councils and Colleges of Consultors," CLSA Proceedings 49 (1987) 210; and Wijlens, 181. Other commentators presume the members of the group are physically present. See, for example, Luigi Chiapetta, Il Codice de Diritto

The central question seems to be whether members "are present" (*sunt praesentes*) only when they are physically there, or whether they "are present" when they are participating through electronic means which allow them to hear and share in the discussion. Some might argue that being physically present provides an opportunity beforehand to informally discuss the matter being considered and that there are certain psychological advantages to being physically present especially if there was a disinclination to give consent (e.g., strength in numbers). Others might counter that the informal discussions begin long before a group gathers, but the discussion that is important is the one actually during the meeting where the free exchange of ideas and arguments can convince or change minds, and that the sense of detachment and anonymity provided by electronic means of communication offer their own psychological advantages to offer an opinion contrary to the desire of a superior (e.g., the shield of distance to say difficult things). This type of interchange, however, ignores the requirement of members of the group to offer their opinions sincerely,[6] even if they are not the ones hoped for by a superior. Such an interchange also ignores a more fundamental question of what "being present" truly means. Is being able to hear and to voice one's opinions during the meeting with full access to all the information being presented—whether documentary, audio or visual—sufficient to constitute "presence," or is actually being physically there constitutive to being present in order to give consent?

Interestingly, in the United States of America, boards of directors of both business corporations and nonprofit corporations are allowed to be present and participate at meetings of the boards through electronic means.[7] These boards

---

Canonico: Commento giuridico-pastorale, 2nd ed. (Rome: Edizioni Dehoniane, 1996) I:195, no. 894; Mendonça, 58-64.

[5] See Hill, 91; Richard A. Hill, S.J., "The Role of Councils," Review for Religious 45 (1986) 140-144; Pree, 485; Thériault, I:810; and Woestman, 19-21.

[6] See c. 127, §3.

[7] See Committee on Corporation Laws of the Section of Business Law of the American Bar Association, Model Business Corporation Act: Annotated, 4th ed. (Chicago, IL: American Bar Association, 2008), §8.20(b), which has been adopted whole or in part in over 30 states, and Subcommittee on the Model Nonprofit Corporation Laws of the Business Law Section of the American Bar Association, Revised Model Nonprofit Corporation Act with Official Comments and Statutory Cross-References (Clifton, NH: Prentice-Hall Law & Business, 1988), §8.20(c), which has been adopted whole or in part by over 20 states (for examples of states adopting these model laws, see Colorado Revised Statutes §7-108-201(2) and §7-128-201(2); Wyoming Statutes §17-16-820(b) and §17-19-820(c)). Individual state corporations statutes should be consulted, because each state makes modifications to proposed model acts; however, the use of electronic means appears to be universally allowed for boards of directors meetings even in states with their own unique legislation (see, for example, California Corporations Code §307(a)(6), §5211(a)(6),

discuss and decide on matters similar in nature to those in canon law which require consent, and the decisions of these corporate boards are deliberative and not merely consultative.

After a preliminary evaluation of whether electronic means can be used to obtain the consent of a group, the Pontifical Council for Legislative Texts, in a private reply, concluded that the matter is not a question about the interpretation of law, but rather application.[8] Being physically present, therefore, does not appear to be constitutive to being able to give consent; however, being physically present can be required by the authority responsible for applying the law. Each Roman dicastery, therefore, in the matters subject to it, has the ability to determine whether participation by electronic means is permissible. The Congregation for the Clergy does not permit electronic means,[9] and the other dicasteries appear to follow the same application of the law.

Electronic means of communication, therefore, when particular or proper law allow, can be used when counsel is being sought. When a matter is subject to the Holy See, electronic means cannot be used when consent is being sought. However, when a matter is not subject to the Holy See, electronic means can be used to obtain consent, provided the ecclesiastical authority judges it applicable.

Rev. Thomas E. Cronkleton, Jr., J.C.D.

---

§7211(a)(6) and 9211(a)(6); Delaware Code Title 8, Chapter 1, §141(f); New York Consolidated Laws, Business Corporations §708(c) and Not-For-Profit Corporations §708(c)).

[8] Pontifical Council for Legislative Texts, Private Reply, July 20, 2006, Prot. No. 10462/2006.

[9] Congregation for the Clergy, Private Reply, August 7, 2006, Prot. No. 20061951.

CANONS 269, 1°; 281, §2 AND 1274, §1

"PAYING IT FORWARD" OR "PONZI SCHEME"?

When a petition from an older priest to be incardinated is received, a diocesan bishop must grapple with the issues of remuneration and retirement. Similar issues arise when a priest already incardinated in the diocese has been absent for duties outside the diocese for a long period of time and wishes to return. Finally, it may well be that a priest has remained within the territory of the diocese but has worked for an entity not subject to the diocesan bishop. All such priests have in common the fact that they fall within definitions of exclusionary clauses found in particular law or other pertinent documents that make them ineligible for the usual diocesan social assistance should they suffer from illness, incapacity, or old age.

Each such cleric presents a unique set of circumstances financially. Thus, the question arises in light of canons 269, 281 and 1274: What guiding principles ought to be incorporated into particular law and other documents emanating from a diocesan bishop to address these special circumstances? In a similar way, may individualized plans be crafted in accord with canonical equity to make provision for the social assistance necessary for such priests? In these cases, what present and future assets of such priests may be considered in evaluating their capacity to provide for their needs?

OPINION

The 2004 *Directory for the Pastoral Ministry of Bishops* (no. 80) summarizes both the law and the values it protects:

> [Priests] should not be deprived of whatever is necessary to maintain a fitting and worthy quality of life, and the faithful in the diocese should be aware that it is their responsibility to provide for this.
>
> In this regard, the Bishop should concern himself first of all with their *remuneration,* which must be consistent with their circumstances, 'taking into account the nature of their function and the conditions of place and times,' but also ensuring always that 'they can provide for the necessities of their life as well as for the equitable payment of those whose services they need.' In this way, priests will not find themselves having to seek additional income through activities outside their ministry, which might well obscure their chosen state of life and reduce their pastoral and spiritual activity. Steps should also be taken to ensure that they can benefit

> from *social assistance,* 'which provides for their needs suitably if they suffer from illness, incapacity, or old age.'[1]

The questions considered here are about a class of priests more specifically defined as those for whom the time value of money is working against them. They could be those about to be newly incardinated or already incardinated but about to be reintroduced to ministry in the diocese. These priests could receive the standard remuneration and current health benefits without any complication. The problem arises because protections have been built into diocesan funding mechanisms that exclude them from social assistance in the future when they suffer from illness, incapacity, or old age.

This class of priests also includes those who are not specifically excluded but who, as a result of the abstractness in the law, have their situation rendered untenable, inadequate, or unjust.

Perhaps not all dioceses would have a priest that would meet these requisites. The following principles are proposed as the basis of current remuneration and an alternative system of social assistance to meet the needs of such priests who are capable of active ministry for a while and who will too soon suffer from illness, incapacity, or old age.

A significant decree from the Pontifical Council for Legislative Texts[2] provides the best guidance, and is summarized as follows:

> It was explicitly within the *ratio legis* intended by the canonical legislator that he both wished "...to express the unity of ministerial service of the priests incardinated in a diocese and to guarantee an adequate equalization of work and of remuneration between all the priests" (p. 165).

Any document emanating from the authority of a diocesan bishop is equivalent to particular law. Policies, guidelines, and fund and trust documents are all to be interpreted canonically as laws.

The diocesan system in place for the remuneration of an incardinated priest assigned to long-term active ministry in the juridic persons subject to the diocesan bishop, and the provisions made for him when he suffers from illness, incapacity, or old age, is the "standard of care" of priests in a given diocese.

---

[1] Congregation for Bishops, *Directory for the Pastoral Ministry of Bishops*, *Apostolorum Successores*, February 22, 2004 (Vatican City: Libreria Editrice Vaticana, 2004), 89-90.

[2] Pontifical Council for Legislative Texts, Decree, April 29, 2000, Prot. No. 7194/2000, in *Communicationes* 32 (2000) 162-167.

This standard is a baseline against which the financial provision for an incoming or returning priest's fitting and worthy quality of life–both present and future–are to be judged, regardless of his age.

It is not only permitted, but is presumed, that such a priest must cooperate with an assay of his current earnings and future inurnments from the exercise of his priestly ministry. Excluded from this assessment are personal assets, defined as income or future earnings or an entitlement to which he might have a right as long as it comes from strictly personal savings and investments, inheritance or beneficial income.

Such a priest is required for the common good to request all pensions and benefits whatsoever to which he may have a current or future right or interest. From time to time priests may propose that they will not participate in the Social Security system. Not only would these retirement benefits be lost but others that hinge upon them. Thus, it must be clearly indicated in particular law and carefully communicated to the clergy that no priest may opt out of Social Security (FICA) or any other retirement system since noncompliance would ultimately be a grave injustice affecting the common good.

"Paying it Forward"

Those incoming or returning priests are expected by the canonical legislator to engage in reciprocity for the common good based on the principle that a necessary equality should exist among the priests of the diocese and none should take from the common funds what they collect or could collect if they requested it from other entities. Thus, either by particular law or by a memorandum of understanding an incoming or returning priest is to facilitate, in cooperation with diocesan personnel, a careful review of his assets from every other entity except from his personal goods in the strict sense. A comparison is to be made and an equitable financial plan is to be devised so that such a priest will have the same remuneration and future social assistance that is at all times equal to the "standard of care" of those who have continuously served within the diocese. Whatever assets (exclusive of personal goods) are above that baseline, the surplus is to be left in the common resources of the diocesan pool for the common good.

"Ponzi Scheme"

Conversely, after an incoming or returning priest endures the same scrutiny, his assets may not meet the "standard of care." Then special provision must be made so that when he suffers from illness, incapacity, or old age, the funds will be available for him to have that same "standard of care" afforded all clergy. Usually, assignment to a parish or other duty will provide for current remuneration and health needs. So that the individual will have the social assistance necessary at some future date when he suffers from illness, incapacity, or old age, it will require special provisions outside the usual system of compensation. It might be that the sending diocese, religious order, or ecclesiastical entities for which he has worked may be of assistance in contributing to a fund, insurance policies or other financial mechanisms that will provide for such a priest.

The canonical legislator expects a legitimate "Ponzi Scheme" when the exclusionary clause of diocesan particular law or other documents emanating from the diocesan bishop exclude priests who suffer from illness, incapacity, or old age. Funds, even from current contributors, must be made available to these unqualified beneficiaries. If the funds cannot be taken from the diocesan priests' retirement fund for civilly valid reasons, then they are due nonetheless from other sources.

Before the incardination of an older priest or reintroduction of an already incardinated priest, it is prudent to undertake financial planning and prepare for the day he suffers from illness, incapacity, or old age.

Rev. Bruce Miller, J.C.L.

CANON 447

DIOCESAN OBLIGATION TO PAY EPISCOPAL CONFERENCE ASSESSMENT

Can a diocesan bishop refuse to pay his portion of the expenses of the episcopal conference, or at least refuse to pay the increase in levies from the previous financial year?

OPINION

The Second Vatican Council established episcopal conferences in *Christus Dominus,* no. 38. Episcopal conferences are described in similar words in canon 447:

> A conference of bishops, a permanent institution, is a group of bishops of some nation or certain territory who jointly exercise certain pastoral functions for the Christian faithful of their territory in order to promote the greater good which the Church offers to humanity, especially through forms and programs of the apostolate fittingly adapted to the circumstances of time and place, according to the norm of law.

The canon describes the episcopal conference as a "permanent institution," in contrast to other institutions, such as provincial councils, which meet occasionally. Since an episcopal conference is a permanent institution, it is able to ensure an ongoing supervision and coordination of some pastoral activities.

Since the promulgation of the 1983 *Code of Canon Law,* issues have arisen about the relationship between the episcopal conference and individual diocesan bishops. Pope John Paul II issued the Apostolic Letter *motu proprio, Apostolos suos* on May 21, 1998,[1] and the Congregation for Bishops issued the *Directory for the Pastoral Ministry of Bishops*, *Apostolorum Successores*, on February 22, 2004.[2] Many of the issues were addressed in these documents.

Pope John Paul II emphasized the collegial spirit of episcopal conferences by recalling, in *Apostolos suos*, that "The Lord Jesus constituted the Apostles 'in the form of a college or permanent assembly, at the head of which he

---

[1] Pope John Paul II, Apostolic Letter *motu proprio*, *Apostolos suos*, May 21, 1998, in *Acta Apostolicae Sedis* 90 (1998) 641-658; English translation in *Origins* 28/9 (1998) 152-158.

[2] Congregation for Bishops, *Directory for the Pastoral Ministry of Bishops*, *Apostolorum Successores*, February 22, 2004 (Vatican City: Libreria Editrice Vaticana, 2004).

placed Peter, chosen from amongst them'" (no. 1). The Apostles were not chosen and sent by Jesus independently of one another, but rather as part of the group of the Twelve, as the Gospels make clear by the repeatedly used expression, "one of the Twelve." To all of them together the Lord entrusted the mission of preaching the Kingdom of God, and they were sent by him, not individually, but "two by two." However, *Apostolos suos* is careful in article 12 to point out that "'episcopal collegiality in the strict and proper sense belongs only to the entire College of Bishops, which as a theological subject is indivisible.'" Consequently, *Apostolos suos* article 14 states "Episcopal Conferences constitute a concrete application of the collegial spirit." Their purpose is very clear in *Apostolos suos,* article 4: "These Conferences were set up for specific pastoral purposes, as a means of responding to different ecclesiastical questions of common interest and finding appropriate solutions to them." Therefore, *Apostolos suos* concludes, that "When the Bishops of a territory jointly exercise certain pastoral functions for the good of their faithful, such joint exercise of the episcopal ministry is a concrete application of collegial spirit (*affectus collegialis*), which 'is the soul of the collaboration between the Bishops at the regional, national and international levels'" (no. 12). Such collaboration is very important for dealing with governments and civil authorities. Therefore, as indicated by the Second Vatican Council, the Apostolic See grants episcopal conferences "the power to issue *binding norms* on certain matters[3] and to adopt *particular decisions*, which each Bishop should accept faithfully and apply in his diocese."[4]

While *Apostolos suos* is careful to convey that the episcopal conference is not just a gathering of individuals, it clearly upholds the authority of an individual diocesan bishop in article 10: "Equivalent collegial actions cannot be carried out at the level of individual particular Churches or of gatherings of such Churches called together by their respective Bishops. At the level of an individual Church, it is in the name of the Lord that the diocesan Bishop leads the flock entrusted to him, and he does so as the proper, ordinary and immediate Pastor. His actions are strictly personal, not collegial, even when he has a sense of being in communion." Likewise, the *Directory for the Pastoral*

---

[3] Canon 455, §1: "A conference of bishops can only issue general decrees in cases where universal law has prescribed it or a special mandate of the Apostolic See has established it either *motu proprio* or at the request of the conference itself." These decrees according to c. 455, §2 must be passed by a two thirds vote of those members with a deliberative vote, and are not binding until "they have been legitimately promulgated after having been reviewed by the Apostolic See."

[4] *Directory for the Pastoral Ministry of Bishops*, no. 31.

Ministry of Bishops points out that "Episcopal Conferences are intended to be instruments of mutual assistance for Bishops in fulfilling their pastoral responsibilities" (no. 31).

A number of pastoral activities can be entrusted to the bishops of a conference, because of circumstances such as availability of personnel, finances, etc. Examples could be an interdiocesan tribunal, which may in fact be for the territory of an entire episcopal conference (e.g., cc. 1423, 1439), or a national seminary (c. 237, §2). Once these institutions have been mandated or approved by the Apostolic See, their maintenance, provision of personnel and finances are a legal requirement that devolves upon the episcopal conference.

Concerning tribunals, "Norms for Interdiocesan or Regional or Interregional Tribunals" were approved by the Supreme Tribunal of the Apostolic Signatura on December 28, 1970.[5] Article 20 stated: "The same assembly shall decide in what measure or proportion each one of the dioceses shall provide assistance to the respective tribunals of first and second instance, both by supplying suitable priests for the assignments as judges and officers, and by paying a monetary contribution from which as well as from the entrance money of the tribunals the stipends of persons and the costs of each tribunal can be paid."[6] These norms provide a guide for dealing with similar matters in episcopal conference expenditure according to canon 19.

Therefore, when the financial levy is for a matter that the episcopal conference must provide by law, or has been approved by the Apostolic See, each individual bishop must pay his portion of the expenses as agreed upon by a majority of the episcopal conference. When the expenditure approved by the majority of the episcopal conference is not for a pastoral activity required by law, then the individual diocesan bishop is within his rights not to pay the financial levy.

Rev. Brendan Daly, J.C.D.

---

[5] See *Canon Law Digest* 7:920-926.

[6] Supreme Tribunal of the Apostolic Signatura, "Norms for Interdiocesan or Regional or Interregional Tribunals," December 28, 1970, art. 20, in *Canon Law Digest* 7:925.

CANON 520

THE RIGHTS OF A DIOCESAN BISHOP WITH REGARD TO A PARISH ENTRUSTED *PLENO IURE* TO A RELIGIOUS INSTITUTE

There is a parish in my diocese which was entrusted to a religious institute pleno iure *under the 1917 Code of Canon Law. The parish is claiming not to be subject to the same diocesan tax and the same level of financial accountability as other parishes. Is this correct?*

OPINION

The 1983 *Code of Canon Law* no longer contains provisions for entrusting a parish to a religious institute *pleno iure* (in full right). The ability to entrust a parish *pleno iure* to a religious institute was discontinued with the dismantling of the benefice system after the Second Vatican Council.[1]

Under the 1917 *Code of Canon Law*, while a diocesan bishop was competent to entrust a parish to a religious institute, a bishop was not competent to entrust a parish *pleno iure* to a religious institute. This could only be done by the Apostolic See, and was ordinarily handled by the Sacred Congregation of the Council (c. 250 of *CIC*/17). To entrust a parish *pleno iure*, a contract would be drawn up between the diocesan bishop and the religious superior. The contract would be reviewed and approved by the Sacred Congregation of the Council, which then would decree that the parish was entrusted *pleno iure* to the religious institute. Any special privileges for the religious institute would have been established in the written agreement between the diocesan bishop and the religious superior at the time when the parish was entrusted *pleno iure*.

A parish entrusted *pleno iure* did not have a physical person as pastor. The religious institute itself was the pastor, and a parochial vicar was assigned who had all of the usual rights and obligations of a pastor. "If a parish has been united in full law to a religious house, capitular church, or other moral person, a parochial vicar must be constituted who actually conducts the care of souls [and to whom there is] assigned an appropriate share of its proceeds, in the judgment of the Bishop" (c. 471, §1 of *CIC*/17).[2]

---

[1] See Second Vatican Council, Decree on the Ministry and Life of Priests, *Presbyterorum ordinis*, December 7, 1965, no. 20.

[2] Translations of the 1917 *Code of Canon Law* are taken from Edward N. Peters, *The 1917 or Pio-Benedictine Code of Canon Law* (San Francisco: Ignatius Press, 2001).

The religious institute acquired the right to appoint this parochial vicar. "But if it is [united] *in full right*, the parish becomes religious and the Superior can appoint a priest from his own religious [institute] to exercise the care of souls, but it is for the local Ordinary to approve and install him, and he remains under him with regard to jurisdiction, correction, and visitation [and those things] that pertain to the care of souls according to the norm of Canon 631" (c. 1425, §2 of *CIC*/17).

The *pleno iure* union blurred in the minds of many people the distinction between the religious institute and the parish. On this, the Abbo-Hannan commentary on the 1917 Code states: "Authors give a special name to this kind of union, calling it incorporation. But this term is misleading since it implies an absorption or an extinctive union, whereas the union is really a kind of subordinating union."[3] This misunderstanding that a parish joined *pleno iure* was absorbed into the religious institute seems to have been widespread. This frequently led to the mistaken conclusion that the parish became extinct as a separate entity. In truth, there remained two separate entities, although the two were in a special relationship to each other.

As a result of the confusion over the distinction between the parish and the religious institute, there was a common misunderstanding that parishes entrusted *pleno iure* were not under the authority of the diocesan bishop in regard to temporal matters. Exemptions from the diocesan bishop's jurisdiction that belonged to the religious order as an institute of pontifical right were inappropriately extended to include the parish. This seems to have been widespread, despite the clarity of canon 1425, §2 of the 1917 Code, quoted above, and of canon 631, §1, which stated: "Likewise a religious pastor or vicar, even though he exercises ministry in the house or place where the major religious Superiors have their ordinary seat, remains immediately and in every way under the jurisdiction, visitation, and correction of the local Ordinary, not unlike secular pastors, excepting only the observance of the rule."

It is hard to reconcile the confusion over the bishop's rights with the clarity of the canons. Specifically concerning episcopal visitation, the 1917 Code stated: "Subject to ordinary episcopal visitation are persons, things, and pious places, even though exempt, that are contained within the ambit of the diocese, unless it can be proven that there was a special exemption from visitation

---

[3] John A. Abbo and Jerome D. Hannan, *The Sacred Canons* (New York: Herder, 1952), II:657, no. 7.

granted to them by the Apostolic See" (c. 344, §1 of *CIC*/17). Regarding exemption, canons 631, §1 and 1425, §2 of the 1917 Code, quoted above, make it clear that a parish entrusted *pleno iure* is not exempt from episcopal visitation. Furthermore, a 1926 reply of the Pontifical Commission for the Authentic Interpretation of the Code makes it clear that the bishop's right of visitation even extends to any foundations and legacies belonging to such a parish.[4]

The principal benefit, then, to a religious order of having a parish entrusted to it *pleno iure* was related to the income derived from the benefice. Under the benefice system, the pastor (diocesan clergy) had a right to certain income from the parish. This would include income from an endowment and the stole fees. The endowment would be a defined source of revenue that would provide the pastor with regular income (cc. 1409-1410 of *CIC*/17). For example, a rich widow would establish an endowment for her pastor and his successors, leaving money, property that could be leased or other assets that would provide a continued source of income for the pastor from interest or rent. The current office holder would have a right to the profit, but not to the principal.

The benefice would also include stole fees. All stole fees belonged to the pastor by right, regardless of who performed the service (c. 463, §1 of *CIC*/17). For example, if the parochial vicar celebrated a baptism, the stole fee collected on that occasion belonged to the pastor, not to the parochial vicar. The pastor might give him some out of generosity, but he had no obligation to do so. The pastor even had the right to stole fees for his parishioners related to services done at other parishes. For example, if one of his parishioners had his funeral services celebrated at another parish, then the pastor of the other parish had the obligation of remitting at least part of the stole fee back to the proper pastor of the deceased (c. 1236 of *CIC*/17).

Throughout the United States of America, the benefice system properly speaking never truly developed. In the dioceses, there was established either a salary system or other ways of providing income for the pastor. For example, some dioceses established the practice by particular law or custom that the

---

[4] Pontifical Commission for the Authentic Interpretation of the Code, Reply, July 25, 1926, *Acta Apostolicae Sedis* 18 (1926) 393; English translation in *Canon Law Digest* 1:699: "The Code Commission was asked: Whether in virtue of cc. 631, §3; 535, §3, 2°; 533, §1, 3° and 4°, the ordinary of the place has the right to demand an account of the administration of foundations and legacies to a religious parish such as is mentioned in c. 1425, §2. Reply: In the affirmative, without prejudice to the prescription of c. 630, §4, and c. 1550."

pastor had the right to the Christmas and Easter collections in lieu of, or in addition to, a salary paid to him by the parish.

For a parish entrusted *pleno iure* to a religious institute, the benefice income that would ordinarily accrue to a pastor who is a diocesan priest would accrue to the religious institute. This did not include parish income, only what belonged to the benefice (e.g., the endowment and stole fees). Donations given to the offertory collection at Mass belonged to the parish (c. 1536, §1 of *CIC*/17), not to the benefice.

In situations where there was no endowment and no actual benefice, there would have been few financial benefits for a religious institute to have a parish entrusted to it *pleno iure*, unless the original contract gave it special rights. The only other benefit would have been the stole fees. However, the matter of stole fees has been reordered by the 1983 Code, and now such offerings belong to the parish, not to the pastor or the benefice (cc. 531; 1267, §1).

In the 1983 Code, the concept of a "juridic person" was introduced, replacing and clarifying the 1917 Code's concept of a "moral person." Just as a physical person can be the subject of rights and obligations, a juridic person can be the subject of rights and obligations as a legal entity. In the 1983 Code, all doubt has been removed that the parish and the religious institute are two separate juridic persons. Canon 515, §3 recognizes that parishes are juridic persons and canon 634, §1 recognizes religious institutes, provinces, and houses as juridic persons. Furthermore, any doubt about the fact that two separate entities are involved was removed by a February 8, 2000 response of the Pontifical Council for Legislative Texts.

In 1999, a religious institute in Spain took recourse against the general decree of a diocesan bishop to impose a tax on public juridic persons subject to him. The religious institute claimed that a certain parish was entrusted to it *pleno iure* and therefore was not subject to the tax. However, on February 8, 2000 the Pontifical Council for Legislative Texts ruled against the religious institute and in favor of the diocesan bishop.[5] It stated that:

- All parishes, without exception, are distinct public juridic persons, separate from any religious institute to which they have been entrusted in any manner;
- All parishes, without exception, are fully under the jurisdiction of the diocesan bishop;

[5] Pontifical Council for Legislative Texts, Decree, February 8, 2000, no. 4.5, *Communicationes* 32 (2000) 15-23.

- All parishes, without exception, are subject to the same ordinary and proportionate tax;
- The diocesan bishop has the authority to separate a parish which has been entrusted *pleno iure* to a religious institute from that institute[6];
- The religious institute has the right to continue to staff the parish and should enter into an agreement with the diocesan bishop as envisioned in canon 520, §2;
- The religious institute may retain other acquired rights that were a part of the original agreement, except for the right to maintain the parish in a state of *pleno iure* union;
- If an agreement, in accord with canon 520, §2, cannot be reached between the diocesan bishop and the religious superior, recourse is to be taken to competent congregations of the Holy See (presumably the Congregation for Institutes of Consecrated Life and Societies of Apostolic Life and the Congregation for the Clergy).

The stipulation regarding separating the parish from the religious institute is consistent with the desire of canon 520, §1 of the 1983 Code, which states bluntly: "A juridic person is not to be a pastor."

In a situation where a parish has been entrusted *pleno iure* to a religious institute, before a diocesan bishop issues a decree separating the two entities, there needs to be clarity with regard to the ownership of temporal goods. It is necessary to clarify what property, money, and other assets belong to the parish and what belongs to the religious institute. Once issues related to ownership of temporal goods are resolved, then the decree of separation can be issued by the bishop and the details of an agreement regarding the future pastoral staffing of the parish can be worked out.

If there was an endowment established at the time a parish was entrusted *pleno iure* to the religious institute by the Holy See, then the religious institute continues to have a right to the income from the endowment as an acquired right. That endowment would be subject to the canons on pious wills and pious foundations (cc. 1299-1310).

Once the parish is separated, and the diocesan bishop and religious superior enter the agreement described in canon 520, §2, the obligation and

---

[6] The decree states that this interpretation is in accord with the June 25, 1979 response of the Pontifical Commission for the Interpretation of the Decrees of the Second Vatican Council, *Acta Apostolicae Sedis* 71 (1979) 696; English translation in *Canon Law Digest* 9:909; and the August 6, 1966 Apostolic Letter *Ecclesiae Sanctae* I, issued *motu proprio* by Pope Paul VI; English translation in *Canon Law Digest* 6:280.

right of visitation by the diocesan bishop with regard to the parish is broad (cc. 396-398). Visitation is one of the primary ways that the bishop exercises vigilance (c. 392, §2). The bishop's vigilance includes the right to expect financial accountability. The basic limit is that the bishop does not have authority over the internal governance of religious institutes and the religious discipline of the members of the institute (see cc. 397, §2; 586; 678).

In regard to vigilance over temporal goods, canon 1276 states:

> §1. It is for the ordinary to exercise careful vigilance over the administration of all the goods which belong to public juridic persons subject to him, without prejudice to legitimate titles which attribute more significant rights to him.
> §2. With due regard for rights, legitimate customs, and circumstances, ordinaries are to take care of the ordering of the entire matter of the administration of ecclesiastical goods by issuing special instructions within the limits of universal and particular law.

The 2000 decree of the Pontifical Council for Legislative Texts makes it clear that all parishes are subject to the same visitation and vigilance of the diocesan bishop. This was true under the 1917 Code and remains true under the 1983 Code.

Regarding an assessment imposed by the diocesan bishop on parishes, canon 1263 of the 1983 Code states: "After the diocesan bishop has heard the finance council and the presbyteral council, he has the right to impose a moderate tax for the needs of the diocese upon public juridic persons subject to his governance; this tax is to be proportionate to their income...." The 2000 decree of the Pontifical Council for Legislative Texts makes it clear that all parishes, without exception, are subject to the same diocesan tax. While the religious institute may retain rights that it acquired at the time that the parish was entrusted to it *pleno iure*, the parish itself does not retain any rights from having previously been entrusted *pleno iure* to a religious institute. The *pleno iure* union was never meant to give the parish rights, but only to give the religious institute rights. The parish itself was, and is, subject to the full jurisdiction of the diocesan bishop, and is to be taxed like any other parish.

Rev. Mark J. Gantley, J.C.L.

CANONS 868, §1, 1° AND 391

PARTICULAR LAW REQUIRING THE CONSENT OF BOTH PARENTS TO BAPTIZE MINOR CHILDREN

Due to an increase in civil law custodial agreements that require the consent of both parents for any decisions affecting the spiritual upbringing of their minor children, the diocesan general counsel's office has recommended that the diocesan bishop enact a particular law requiring the consent of both parents for the reception of the sacrament of baptism. The bishop has questioned whether such a law would be in accord with canon law. Can you advise?

OPINION

In previous editions of *CLSA Advisory Opinions*, canonists have debated the rights and obligations of *parents* in these unfortunate situations.[1] This case, however, concerns the power of the diocesan bishop to enact particular law for his diocese, and his own obligation to see that the laws enacted comply with the requisite canonical principles.

The right and duty of diocesan bishops to enact particular law is deeply rooted in the theology of episcopal governance (*Lumen Gentium*, no. 27). A bishop's legislative power is an integral part of his ordinary and proper authority. Through the development of particular legislation, the bishop provides for local exigencies not envisioned by the universal legislator, or adapts the general provisions of the universal law to the particular demands of the local church. The *Code of Canon Law* is replete with examples of instances where the promulgation of particular legislation is envisioned by the universal legislator.[2] Diocesan bishops, moreover, are not restricted to the explicit references in the Code for the exercise of their legislative power; as long as the subject matter has not been explicitly reserved to higher ecclesiastical authority, the bishop's ability to legislate may be favorably presumed.[3] In this

---

[1] See, for example, Brendan Daly, "Baptism of Child of Separated Parents," in *Roman Replies and CLSA Advisory Opinions 2002*, eds. F. Stephen Pedone and James I. Donlon (Washington, DC: Canon Law Society of America, 2002), 104-106; and Patricia M. Dugan and Lynda A. Robitaille, "Baptism of Infant Child of Separated Parents," in *Roman Replies and CLSA Advisory Opinions 2004*, eds. F. Stephen Pedone and James I. Donlon (Washington, DC: Canon Law Society of America, 2004), 145-147 and 147-149, respectively.

[2] With respect to the sanctifying office, for example, see canons 838, §4; 844, §5; 874, §1, 2°; 895; 935; 943; 944, §2; 951, §1; 956; 1002; 1032, §2; 1121, §1; 1177, §3; 1182; 1243; and 1248, §2.

[3] See Congregation for Bishops, *Directory for the Pastoral Ministry of Bishops, Apostolorum Successores* (Vatican City: Libreria Editrice Vaticana, 2004), no. 67, b. For a concise analysis of

way, the power of the local bishop to enact particular law for his diocese is more permissive than the legislative authority granted in the Code to episcopal conferences, which is, by its very nature, restrictive (c. 455).

In the case at hand, the universal law of the Church already expressly provides for the consent needed to baptize infants licitly in the Church. While the Code presumes, and in a sense prefers, that two Catholic parents will be presenting their infant for baptism (*parentes consentiant*), canon 868, §1, 1° stipulates that only one parent (or, indeed, a guardian who has been appointed to see to the spiritual care of the child) need consent to the conferral.[4] The stated minimum in law for such consent is of long-standing tradition in the Church, and covers well the cases of children of single parents (see c. 877, §2), or a Catholic parent who is in a mixed or disparity of cult marriage (see c. 1125).[5] Since the Church believes in the fundamental necessity of baptism for salvation (c. 849; *Catechism of the Catholic Church*, no. 1257), the universal law's provision allowing for the consent of only one parent for its licit conferral allows for the greatest possible latitude for the child to receive the grace conferred in baptism.

Canonical commentators on the parallel canon in the 1917 *Code of Canon Law* (c. 750, §2, 1°) observed that the universal law's provision for the consent needed to administer baptism explicitly accounts for cases where one parent expressly opposes it. H. A. Ayrinhac, for example, explained that: "This rule holds … when only one of the parents or tutors presents the child and the other opposes the baptism. The right of the one who asks for the sacrament, as more in conformity with the law of God and the interests of the child, prevails over that of the other."[6] It was the common estimation of canonists that the norm respects the natural right of parents to request baptism, but, more importantly,

---

the legislative competence of the diocesan bishop, see Thomas J. Green, "The Pastoral Governance Role of the Diocesan Bishop: Foundations, Scope and Limitations," *The Jurist 49* (1989) 484-486, 499-500.

[4] The provision of c. 868, §1, 1°, moreover, applies only to ordinary circumstances. In cases where danger of death exists, the Code permits the administration of baptism even against the will of both parents (c. 868, §2).

[5] In canon law, moreover, children become increasingly less dependent on their parents for the consent needed to receive baptism. For example, a fourteen year old child can theoretically request baptism on his or her own initiative (see cc. 111, §2; 1478, §3), a noted exception in the Code to the general norm prescribed in c. 98, §2.

[6] H.A. Ayrinhac, *Legislation on the Sacraments in the New Code* (New York: Longmans, Green and Co., 1928), 28.

the supernatural right of the child to receive it.[7] It was for this reason, that canonists commenting on the 1917 Code explicitly included this norm on lists of "matters entirely outside of particular legislation."[8]

Ultimately, the pastoral governance of the diocesan bishop is to serve the mission of the Church and the salvation of souls. A local law that would require both parents to consent to the baptism of their minor children would be more restrictive than the universal law of the Church, possibly amounting to an improper derogation exceeding the legislative authority granted to bishops in virtue of canons 391 and 838, §4.

While the enactment of a particular law, as recommended by the general counsel's office, is not advised on canonical grounds, because of the frequency of the noted occurrences within the diocese, the bishop may wish to consider developing a uniform policy that can assist pastoral ministers in making prudential judgments in cases where parents do not agree on the reception of baptism for their minor children, or where civil law obligations explicitly stipulate arrangements in this regard (c. 1689). A policy would be a more appropriate vehicle to outline the various circumstances that might suggest a delay in the conferral of the sacrament, or where additional permissions on the local level may be needed (as is provided in the universal law, for example, with regard to certain marriages, c. 1071, §1, 2°). In this way, the bishop will not only fulfill his obligation "to endeavor constantly that the Christian faithful entrusted to his care grow in grace through the celebration of the sacraments" (c. 387), but he will also "promote the common discipline of the whole Church and ... the observance of all ecclesiastical laws" (c. 392, §1).

Siobhan M. Verbeek, J.C.L.

---

[7] See, for example, P. Chas. Augustine, O.S.B., *A Commentary on the Code of Canon Law* (St. Louis, MO: B. Herder Book Co., 1920), IV:54: "This rule is ... based upon the *favor fidei*, which dictates that the supernatural right should prevail over the natural."

[8] See, for example, Edward Roelker, "Particular Legislation and the Term '*Saltem*' in the Code of Canon Law," *The Jurist* 14 (1954) 392.

Canon 869

CELEBRATION OF PENANCE BY A CANDIDATE BEING CONDITIONALLY BAPTIZED

An inquiry has come in regarding the case of a woman who is a candidate for reception into the full communion of the Catholic Church, and whose baptism in a Protestant church is doubtful. When conditional baptism is administered to the candidate, should the sacrament of penance be recommended prior to the candidate's reception?

OPINION

This case ultimately concerns the ecclesial status of a candidate who has been conditionally baptized, and it raises several related pastoral and canonical questions. The first of these has to do with conditional baptism itself. Canon 869 provides detailed rules on conditional baptism that are worth recalling:

> §1. If there is a doubt whether a person has been baptized or whether baptism was conferred validly, and the doubt remains after a serious investigation, baptism is to be conferred conditionally.
> §2. Those baptized in a non-Catholic ecclesial community must not be baptized conditionally unless after an examination of the matter and the form of the words used in the conferral of baptism and a consideration of the intention of the baptized adult person and the minister of the baptism, a serious reason exists to doubt the validity of the baptism.
> §3. If in the cases mentioned in §§ 1 and 2 the conferral or validity of the baptism remains doubtful, baptism is not to be conferred until after the doctrine of the sacrament of baptism is explained to the person to be baptized, if an adult, and the reasons of the doubtful validity of the baptism are explained to the person or, in the case of an infant, to the parents.

Presuming that the procedure of this canon has been followed, and that the doubt about the validity of the baptism has not been resolved, the candidate should be conditionally baptized as early as possible after carefully explaining to her the reason why this is necessary. According to the particular law of the United States Conference of Catholic Bishops (USCCB), the conditional baptism of a candidate "must be celebrated privately rather than at a public liturgical assembly of the community and with only those limited rites which the diocesan bishop determines."[1] This should be done with minimal ceremony (the water and Trinitarian formula often would suffice), not only because the Protestant baptism may have been valid, but also to respect ecumenical sensitivities and to avoid triumphalism.

If the woman had not been validly baptized in the Protestant confession, the conditional baptism will now be effective and she will be a Catholic, but there is no way of knowing this because of the unresolved doubt. In practice, her status continues to be that of a baptized non-Catholic in preparation for reception into full communion. Part of this preparation is the celebration of the sacrament of penance. After baptism, which is the "gateway" to the other sacraments (c. 849), the candidate is capable of validly receiving absolution in the sacrament of penance (see c. 842, §1). While a non-Catholic candidate is not subject to canon law (c. 11), nor is she bound by the merely ecclesiastical law requiring confession of grave sin before receiving Holy Communion (c. 916), she is bound by the divine law[2] that one must be in the state of grace to receive Holy Communion worthily and efficaciously (requiring minimally an act of perfect contrition). Insofar as she seeks reception into full communion, moreover, she *binds herself* to accept the canonical requirements for reception, one of which is the celebration of the sacrament of reconciliation prior to the reception. The liturgical law states: "If the profession and reception take place within Mass, the candidate, attentive to her own personal condition, should confess her sins, after informing the confessor of her impending reception. Any approved confessor may hear this confession."[3] Regarding this requirement, the particular law of the USCCB states:

> The celebration of the sacrament of reconciliation with candidates for reception into full communion is to be carried out at a time prior to and distinct from the celebration of the rite of reception. As part of the formation of such candidates, they should be encouraged in the frequent celebration of this sacrament.[4]

---

1 National Conference of Catholic Bishops, National Statutes for the Catechumenate, November 11, 1986, no. 37, in *Rite of Christian Initiation of Adults* (RCIA), trans. International Commission on English in the Liturgy, Inc. (Chicago: Liturgy Training Publications, 1988), 369.

2 1 Cor 11:29; Council of Trent, sess. XIII, cap. 7.

3 Ordo admissionis valide iam baptizatorum in plenam communionem Ecclesiae catholicae, no. 9, Appendix to Ordo initiationis Christianae adultorum, editio typica, January 6, 1972 (Vatican City: Typis Polyglottis Vaticanis, 1972); trans. John M. Huels. For the International Commission on English in the Liturgy's (ICEL) translation of the same text, see RCIA, 482. I am not in agreement with the entirety of this translation, particularly the words attenta sua personali condicione, which ICEL renders "according to his or her own conscience."

4 National Conference of Catholic Bishops, National Statutes for the Catechumenate, no. 36.

The rite of reception into the full communion of the Catholic Church is preferably celebrated at a Sunday Eucharist with parishioners present.[5] In the course of the rite, the woman will be confirmed and receive first Eucharist. In virtue of their pastoral office, the pastor and the parochial vicar have the faculty by law to confirm those being received into full communion who have not yet been validly confirmed (c. 883, 2°). According to the USCCB's particular law: "The confirmation of such candidates for reception should not be deferred, nor should they be admitted to the Eucharist until they are confirmed."[6] The reception of the sacraments of confirmation and the Eucharist are required for full Christian initiation (c. 842, §2).

John M. Huels, J.C.D.

---

5 Ibid., no. 32.
6 Ibid., no. 35.

CANON 893

PARENTS AS CONFIRMATION SPONSORS

The office of sponsor has a long tradition in the Catholic Church, dating probably from the middle of the second century.[1] *The practice of parents acting as sponsors for their children was common in the fourth century, as a Letter of Saint Augustine to Bishop Boniface indicates.*[2] *However, by the ninth century, Church Councils, such as those of Munich and Arles in 813, forbade parents to be sponsors at the baptism of their children. Canons 765 and 795 of the 1917* Code of Canon *Law also forbade parents to be sponsors at the baptism or confirmation of their children. How is this matter treated in the 1983* Code of Canon Law*?*

OPINION

The legislation of the 1917 *Code of Canon Law* concerning the role of parents as sponsors of their children at baptism or confirmation is repeated in the 1983 *Code of Canon Law*:

> Can. 874 §1. To be permitted to take on the function of sponsor [at baptism] a person must....
>
> 5° not be the father or mother of the one to be baptized.
>
> Can. 893 §1. To perform the function of sponsor [at confirmation], a person must fulfill the conditions mentioned in can. 874 [for sponsors at baptism].
>
> §2. It is desirable to choose as sponsor the one who undertook the same function in baptism.

The law clearly states that the requirements to be a sponsor at confirmation are the same as those to be a sponsor at baptism. However, the *Rite of Confirmation*, promulgated on August 22, 1971,[3] includes a recommendation that the baptismal godparent also be the sponsor at confirmation, and allows for parents to "present" their children for confirmation:

> This change expresses more clearly the relationship between baptism and confirmation and also makes the function and responsibility of the sponsor more effective.

---

[1] Joseph Vicecomes, *Observationes de antiques Baptismi Ritibus ac Ceremoniis* (Parisiis, 1618), lib. 1, cap. 30, q. 1, no. 3.

[2] Richard J. Kearney, *Sponsors at Baptism According to the Code of Canon Law* (Washington, DC: The Catholic University of America, 1925), 52.

[3] *Acta Apostolicae Sedis* 63 (1971) 657-664.

> Nonetheless the choice of a special sponsor for confirmation is not excluded. Even the parents themselves may present their children for confirmation. It is for the local Ordinary to determine diocesan practice in the light of local circumstances.[4]

William H. Woestman, O.M.I. points out that some interpreted this text of the *Praenotanda* of the *Rite of Confirmation* to mean that parents could be sponsors for their child being confirmed. The text says nothing about being sponsors, but only that parents can "present" their children for confirmation.[5]

In 1983, the Congregation for Sacraments and Divine Worship published a *Documentorum explanatio* pointing out that canon 893 clearly states that parents cannot be sponsors:

> From what has been said, it is clear that parents and the godparents exercise different functions in the sacrament of confirmation. For this reason, parents may present their children according to the indicated rubric even though they cannot be admitted to the function of godparent as this function would not add anything to their duty as parents.[6]

In his commentary on canon 893, Kevin Hart claims that

> there is a contradiction between the code which states that parents cannot be their children's confirmation sponsors and the *Rite* which states expressly that they can serve as sponsors...
>
> In the last redaction of the 1980 schema the contradiction between the draft code and *Rite* was brought to the attention of the Commission for the Revision of the Code in a report submitted by four consultors. These consultors argued that the canon treating the requirements for sponsors had to be amended to allow parents to be confirmation sponsors for the children and to harmonize the draft code with the *Rite of Confirmation*.[7]

Hart goes on to argue that responses from the Commission for the Revision of the Code are not authoritative interpretations. Authoritative or authentic interpretations are published in the *Acta Apostolicae Sedis*. Therefore, there is a doubt of law, and "one is free to interpret the rite as allowing parents to act

---

[4] Rite of Confirmation, no. 5, in *The Rites of the Catholic Church*, trans. International Commission on English in the Liturgy (New York: Pueblo Publishing Co, 1976), I:299.
[5] William H. Woestman, O.M.I., *Canon Law of the Sacraments for Parish Ministry* (Ottawa: Faculty of Canon Law Saint Paul University, 2007), 58.
[6] See *Notitiae* 20 (1984) 86; English translation *in Canon Law Digest* 11:202-203.
[7] Kevin T. Hart, Commentary on Canon 893, in *New Commentary on the Code of Canon Law*, eds. John P. Beal, James A. Coriden, and Thomas J. Green (New York: Paulist Press, 2000), 1091.

as sponsors of their children until an authoritative interpretation resolves the conflict."[8] Hart does not address the distinction made between being a sponsor and presenting a child for baptism.

During the process of the revision of the Code, there had been requests, such as from the Australian Bishops' Conference, that parents should not be forbidden to act as sponsors. Four consultors proposed that parents not be prohibited from acting as sponsors at the confirmation of their children.[9] These requests were rejected by the Commission for the Revision of the Code, which pointed out the misunderstanding of the sponsor's role, which was to support the parents in carrying out their responsibilities and duties and, if necessary, supplement the failures of the parents and assist them.

Canon 17 makes it clear that "Ecclesiastical laws must be understood in accord with the proper meaning of the words considered in their text and context." There was confusion over the meaning of what "parents presenting their children" meant. In any case, canon 2 states that "liturgical laws in force until now retain their force unless one of them is contrary to the canons of the Code." There is no need for an authentic interpretation in the *Acta Apostolicae Sedis*, since the law is clear and parents cannot be sponsors of their children when they are confirmed.

Rev. Brendan Daly, J.C.D.

---

[8] *New Commentary on the Code of Canon Law*, 1092.
[9] *Communicationes* 15 (1983) 189.

Canons 945-958

DIOCESAN PRACTICES CONCERNING MASS OFFERINGS

Our diocese is considering implementing a new practice concerning Mass offerings. The proposed practice would have all Mass offerings deposited into the parish operational account as ordinary parish income. Celebrants would no longer receive the Mass offerings, but would receive an increase in their monthly remuneration which would be commensurate with the money priests would receive for celebrating one Mass per day. If priests offer more than one Mass daily, or if they do not offer Mass on every day, there would be no change in their monthly remuneration. Also, aware of the infinite salvific power of each Mass, the policy will allow numerous intentions for any Mass, and the faithful will be informed of this by an announcement in the diocesan newspaper.

Several priests favor this proposal because it would provide all priests with the same monthly remuneration, and it would no longer appear that they are being "paid" to offer Mass. Would this proposal be permitted by canon law?

OPINION

This situation raises several important issues concerning Mass offerings: (1) the right of a priest to receive an offering (c. 945, §1); (2) the right of the faithful to have separate Masses applied for their single offerings (c. 948); and (3) the expectation that Mass offerings are not subject to any diocesan tax (c. 1263). To answer the question adequately, attention must be given to each of these issues.

1 – Mass Offerings are to be Given to the Celebrant

Canon 945, §1 says, "In accord with the approved practice of the Church, any priest celebrating or concelebrating is permitted to receive an offering to apply the Mass for a specific intention." The priest has a right to receive the Mass offering, even though it is "recommended earnestly" that he celebrate Mass for the intentions of the Christian faithful, especially the needy, even if he does not receive an offering (c. 945, §2).

A priest may retain only one Mass offering per day, except on Christmas. If he offers more than one Mass on a given day, he is to transfer the offerings which he received for the additional Masses to the purposes prescribed by the ordinary,[1] although he may have some recompense "by reason of an extrinsic title" (i.e., to cover the costs of remitting the additional offerings) (c. 951, §1). If he *concelebrates* a second Mass on a given day, he cannot receive a Mass offering for it "under any title" (c. 951, §2).

Mass offerings may be accepted by a priest personally, but he may not accept more offerings than he can satisfy within a year (c. 953). He may entrust an entire Mass offering to another acceptable priest who is above suspicion, and he is obliged to see to the celebration of the Mass until he learns that the recipient priest has accepted the offering (c. 955, §1). Once he has accepted a Mass offering, a priest is obliged to offer the Mass for the intention even if the offering is lost through no fault of his own (c. 949).

Mass offerings may also be accepted by a church or oratory. If more Masses are asked to be celebrated there than can be done, the Masses can be celebrated elsewhere unless the donor has expressed a contrary intention (c. 954). Administrators of pious causes and those clergy or laity in any way responsible to see to the celebrations of Masses are to hand over their ordinary Mass obligations which have not been satisfied within a year, in the manner determined by the same ordinary (c. 956).[2]

From these several canons, it is obvious that the Mass offering is to be given to the priest who celebrates the Mass, whether the Mass offering is given directly to him or to another who is to deliver it to him.[3]

2 – Mass Offerings for Separate Masses

Canon 948 is quite clear: "Separate Masses are to be applied for the intentions of those for whom a single offering, though small, has been given and accepted." If the amount of money for the application of Masses is given without any indication of the number of Masses to be celebrated, unless the donor's intention is legitimately presumed to be otherwise, the number of Masses is to be computed based on the offering of the place where the donor

---

[1]The ordinary should clearly specify the purposes to which the priest is to give the Mass offering which he has satisfied but cannot retain. He may, for example, select to direct that such offerings are assigned to the "Institute for Clergy Support" identified in canon 1274, §1 (see cc. 1272; 1303, §2).

[2] See canon 1308 (on the reduction of Mass offerings assigned to a pious foundation) and canon 1309 (on the transfer of Mass offerings assigned to the same).

[3] Mass offerings belong to the priest who celebrates or concelebrates the Mass, and are unable to be treated like the sacramental offerings treated in canon 1264, 2°.

resides (c. 950).[4] The amount of a Mass offering is set by the provincial bishops for both diocesan and religious priests; priests may accept a larger offering but not require a larger offering, unless it is given voluntarily (c. 952).

Thus, the general norm is: "one offering, one Mass." On February 22, 1991, however, the Congregation for the Clergy issued a decree entitled *Mos iugiter*, which allows a priest to offer one Mass for which he has received several Mass offerings. A Mass for "collective intentions" may be offered only under very strict conditions: namely, the faithful making the individual offerings must agree to a Mass for their intention being celebrated with other intentions; the priest may retain only the amount for a single Mass set by the provincial bishops and must remit the excess money to the purposes prescribed by the ordinary, as required by canon 951, §1 (see c. 946); and the faithful are to be informed of the time and place of a Mass celebrated with "collective" intentions, which is not to occur more than twice a week.

Priests are to keep in mind that this practice is an exception to the norm of canon 948, which states clearly: "Separate Masses are to be applied for the intentions of those for whom a single offering, although small, has been given and accepted." Priests with surplus offerings are to forward them to other priests (see c. 955) or to their own ordinary (c. 956).[5] Diocesan bishops are to

---

[4] Interest accrued on Mass offerings need not be used for Masses. The interest may be applied for any purpose determined by the recipient of the offerings. See Paul L. Golden, C.M. "Mass Offerings Held in an Interest Bearing Account," in *Roman Replies and CLSA Advisory Opinions 2007*, eds. Joseph J. Koury and Siobhan M. Verbeek (Washington, DC: Canon Law Society of America, 2007), 78.

Francis G. Morrisey, O.M.I. discusses "money left to parishes in a will for the celebration of Masses. In order to provide for respect of the intentions of the donors, yet at the same time take into account our theology relating to the infinite value of the Mass, in some dioceses bishops have established a policy to the effect that if the number of Masses is not specified in the will, and if the amount available for the celebration of Masses is more than thirty times the diocesan offering, then the sum is to be divided by thirty (in line with the former 'month's mind Masses'); the celebrant receives the ordinary offering in the diocese, and the rest goes to the parish or institution that was the beneficiary. Such a policy would have to be issued before a will is received and the executors notified accordingly when they present the request for Masses. If the number of Masses is indicated in the will and the bequest is accepted, then, of course, the intention has to be honored. At times, a percentage of what remains is taxed to provide for the continuing education of priests, and so forth." See Francis G. Morrisey, O.M.I., "Acquiring Temporal Goods for the Church's Mission," *The Jurist* 56 (1996) 595.

See also John M. Huels, "Indeterminate Mass Obligations," in *Roman Replies and CLSA Advisory Opinions 2007*, eds. Joseph J. Koury and Siobhan M. Verbeek (Washington, DC: Canon Law Society of America, 2007), 79-80.

[5] See Congregation for the Clergy, Decree, *Mos iugiter*, February 22, 1991, *Acta Apostolicae Sedis* 83 (1991) 443-446; English translation in *Origins* 20 (1990-1991) 705-706. For extensive commentaries on *Mos iugiter* see Gilberto Agustoni, Commentary on the Decree, in *Origins* 20 (1990-1991) 706-707; and Julio Manzanares, "De stipendio pro missis ad intentionem 'collectivam' celebratis iuxta decretum 'Mos iugiter,'" *Periodica* 80 (1991) 579-608.

see to the observance of the norms of *Mos iugiter* by all priests, secular and religious.

3 – Mass Offerings and Diocesan Taxation

Mass offerings are not subject to the diocesan taxation permitted by canon 1263. They are not considered part of parish income.

The 1917 *Code of Canon Law* permitted the ordinary to impose a "foundation tax" for the good of the diocese or of the patrons of a church upon benefices and other ecclesiastical institutes subject to him at the time of the their foundation or consecration (c. 1506 of *CIC*/1917). This canon, identified as a source of canon 1263 of the 1983 *Code of Canon Law*, expressly prohibits taxation of Mass offerings, whether manual or foundational.

Early in the process of developing canon 1263, the *coetus De bonis Ecclesiae temporalibus* suggested that the prohibition on taxing Mass offerings be situated elsewhere in the Code.[6] Throughout the various drafts of what became canon 1263, however, the prohibition on taxing Mass offerings was always expressly stated, even in the 1982 draft which was presented to Pope John Paul II by the Plenary Commission for the revision of the *Code of Canon Law*.[7] It was during the subsequent papal consultation that the prohibition was extracted.

Nonetheless, Mass offerings are not subject to taxation. This is stated explicitly in canon 1012 of the *Code of Canons of the Eastern Churches*, the legislation which corresponds to canon 1263 of the Code for the Latin Church. Further, a decree of the Pontifical Council for Legislative Texts concerning diocesan taxes, dated February 8, 2000, explains that Mass offerings are not subject to the diocesan tax.[8]

---

[6] *Communicationes* 5 (1973) 95.

[7] Pontifical Commission for the Revision of the Code of Canon Law, *Codex Iuris Canonici, Schema Novissimum post consultationem S.R.E. Cardinalium, episcoporum conferentiarum, dicasteriorum curiae romanae, universitatum facultatumque ecclesiarum necnon superiorum institutorum vitae consecratae recognitum, iuxta placita Patrum Commissionis deinde emendatum atque Summo pontifici praesentatum* (Vatican City: Typis Polyglottis Vaticanis, 1982), c. 1263.

[8] Pontifical Council for Legislative Texts, *Decretum, De recursu super congrugentia inter legem particularem et normam codicalem* [Recourse against a general decree which establishes a diocesan *tributum*], February 8, 2000, *Communicationes* 32 (2000) 23. See also Eugene J. Fitzsimmons, "Mass Offerings and Stole Fees," in *Church Finance Handbook*, eds. Kevin E. McKenna, Lawrence A. DiNardo, and Joseph W. Pokusa (Washington, DC: Canon Law Society of America, 1999), 63-76.

4–Mass Offerings Kept by the Parish, Increase in Priests' Remuneration

In the minds of some, treating Mass offerings as given to the parish may be considered to parallel the practice of giving offerings on the occasion of the celebration of the sacraments and sacramentals to the parish, rather than to the priest. Canon 531 says that offerings given on the occasion of some parochial function, even if performed by someone not assigned to the parish, are to be placed into the parish account, unless the donor's contrary intention is clear. The canon requires the diocesan bishop to consult the presbyteral council before he establishes prescripts to specify the allocation of these offerings and to remunerate the clerics who perform the parochial function. Canon 551 says that the norm of canon 531 applies to parochial vicars assigned to a parish. Neither canon 531 nor canon 551, however, applies to Mass offerings.

On March 17, 1981, an archbishop in the United States of America sought an indult allowing him to assign stole fees and Mass offerings to the parish or institution. This proposal was presented by his presbyteral council and approved by the college of consultors in a desire to provide a just and equitable remuneration for priests. On April 29, 1981, the Sacred Congregation for the Clergy replied that stole fees could be remitted to the parish, in accord with the discipline of *Eccelsiae Sanctae,* no. 8. The prefect added: "We cannot, however, grant the requested indult to assign Mass stipends to the parish or institution where the Sacraments are celebrated, since it is part of the letter and the spirit of the law, to give the Mass stipend directly to the celebrant (can. 824 and can.1506 C.I.C., confirmed by the rather recent Motu Proprio *Firma in Traditione*, [*AAS* 66 (1974) 308-311].)"[9]

If a diocese were to offer priests the option of an increase in monthly remuneration in return for surrendering their Mass offerings, this arrangement would need to be entirely voluntary–that is, it would need to be an option which each priest may freely either select or reject. If a priest chooses to surrender Mass offerings in return for a set monthly remuneration, in effect he would be freely giving the Mass offerings to the parish and in turn receiving a set remuneration. Seemingly, this arrangement would not contradict the letter or spirit of the law concerning Mass offerings. The Mass offerings would still be the property of the priest, who can dispose of them however he would wish. Unlike the indult which was denied in 1981 by the Sacred Congregation for

---

[9]Reported in *Roman Replies and CLSA Advisory Opinions 1984*, eds. William A. Schumacher and Richard A. Hill, S.J. (Washington, DC: Canon Law Society of America, 1984), 2.

the Clergy and would have been mandatory throughout the archdiocese, this arrangement would be voluntary–freely chosen or not by each priest. Given the complexity of this (e.g., the need to customize the arrangement for each priest, including visiting priests who celebrate Mass at the parish on occasion), one may question its practical advantage.

In light of the above, and in answer to the question posed, one concludes that Mass offerings always belong to the priest-celebrant, whether they are accepted personally by him or by a church or oratory and given to him when he celebrates the Mass. Nothing prevents him, however, from giving them back to the parish freely in return for a set remuneration, though such an arrangement is cumbersome in practice and could cause confusion that Mass offerings are treated in law analogously to offerings for other sacraments and sacramentals. Even if Mass offerings are received by a parish or oratory, however, they are not subject to diocesan taxation. They are not ordinary parish income. Further, though the law permits the offering of a single Mass for "collective intentions," such a practice is to be considered exceptional. It may not occur more than twice a week, and individual donors must be willing to join their intention with the others to form the "collective intentions" for the single Mass.

Rev. Msgr. John A. Renken, J.C.D.

CANON 1041, 5°

VASECTOMY AS AN IRREGULARITY FOR RECEIVING ORDERS

The diocesan vicar for clergy has requested an opinion on whether a vasectomy constitutes an irregularity for receiving orders, in accord with canon 1041, 5°; if so, under what circumstances might a candidate be dispensed from this irregularity?

OPINION

Canon 17 instructs that "laws must be read and understood in accord with the proper meaning of the words considered in their text and context." Of principal importance to this question, therefore, is the meaning of the word "mutilation" in canon 1041, 5°. In a Thomistic sense, mutilation is best understood as an intentional act which limits a person's capacity for acting in some authentically human way. The intentional severing of a limb, for example, limits a person's capacity to act and thus would constitute mutilation.[1] The contrast to this principle is the maiming of a particular limb or body part because its presence causes undue harm to the rest of the body; such an act would not be considered mutilation. One example of this would be a therapeutic orchiectomy, or testicular removal, undertaken out of medical necessity and not for the purpose of sterilization. Such incidental sterilization is not the subject of this consideration.

Obviously, voluntarily rendering oneself completely sterile constitutes a significant limitation on the capacity to act in an authentically and fully human way; thus, if sterilization is directly and principally intended by some medical procedure, such as vasectomy, this would constitute mutilation. Brian Dunn argues extensively for this position in his 2004 treatment of the question.[2] Dunn suggests that a procedure that is directly intended to sterilize is a grave bodily mutilation insofar as it renders some organ of the body radically unable to act. He acknowledges, however, the theological ambiguity of the term mutilation. This ambiguity, it seems, is a principle cause for the diversity of

---

[1] Joseph Rickaby, S.J., *Aquinas Ethicus: The Moral Theology of St. Thomas, A Translation of the Principal Portions of the Second Part of the Summa Theologica* (London: Burns and Oates, 1896), 1274.

[2] Brian Dunn, "Does a Vasectomy Constitute an Irregularity to the Sacrament of Orders?," *Studia Canonica* 38 (2004) 481-508.

opinions on the issue of vasectomy and orders.[3] William Varvaro, for example, argued that a canonical understanding of mutilation requires that the severing or harm be done to an external organ of the body.[4]

The conclusion that vasectomy does constitute mutilation seems to be supported by consistent magisterial teaching on vasectomy which, as a means of direct sterilization, is an objectively grave moral evil (see *Catechism of the Catholic Church*, no. 2399, *Humanae Vitae,* no. 14, etc.). Obviously, the morality of vasectomy is not at issue in this consideration, but that direct sterilization is so emphatically condemned by the magisterium does offer some insight into the *mentis legibus* on this question.

Of course, the gravity of vasectomy does not establish that a vasectomy constitutes an irregularity to orders. The quest of malice must also be considered. On this point, Dunn remarks that "This technically precise word...indicates that the mutilation has to be seriously sinful for the person to incur the irregularity, i.e., serious matter, appropriate intention and knowledge."[5] In the case of vasectomy, those who undergo the procedure do so certainly intending the desired outcome, that is, they intend the harm of impeded fertility.

The fact that a woman's health might be imperiled by future pregnancy does not mitigate the objective immorality of undergoing a vasectomy, any more than utilizing prophylactic or pharmaceutical contraceptives is justified by such a circumstance. Such a mitigating factor, though it may lead a person to choose a vasectomy, would not impede the *dolus* of the act since the intention, direct sterilization, is, in a certain sense, what defines the act of vasectomy. Nevertheless, it is essential to recognize that the imputability of the party is a determining factor in assessing the possibility of this irregularity.

In light of these considerations, it seems reasonable to conclude that those candidates for orders who have undergone vasectomies have incurred the irregularity of mutilation established in canon 1041, 5°. If this is the case, the question of appropriate exercise of dispensation must be considered.

---

[3] The diversity of opinions on this subject is evident from the body of scholarly work on both sides of the question. For excellent examples offering substantially different conclusions, see William A. Varvaro, "Irregularity for Receiving Order of Diaconate (Permanent) Following Vasectomy," in *CLSA Advisory Opinions 1984-1993*, ed. Patrick J. Cogan, S.A. (Washington, DC: Canon Law Society of America, 1995), 309-311; and William H. Woestman, O.M.I., *The Sacrament of Orders and the Clerical State*, 2nd rev. ed. (Ottawa: Faculty of Canon Law, Saint Paul University, 2001).

[4] Varvaro, 310.

[5] Dunn, 496.

In accord with canon 1047, the local ordinary is able to dispense from the irregularities established in canon 1041, 5°, in public or occult cases, except when the case is reserved to the Apostolic See by virtue of canon 1047, §1. Such reservation can be imagined in a situation in which a candidate for orders has petitioned the tribunal for a declaration of nullity, and it is in that forum that knowledge of the vasectomy arises. Under ordinary circumstances, however, the ordinary is, in accord with canon 87, able to dispense from irregularities whenever he judges that such a dispensation would contribute to the spiritual good of his subjects. There is no prescribed process by which the ordinary must proceed, although canon 90 requires him to undertake some accounting of the case's circumstances before acting. Therefore, the ordinary must initiate any petition for a dispensation with a consideration of the parties' imputability.

It is worth noting that an irregularity is a perpetual impediment. Therefore, one who has incurred an irregularity remains irregular for orders even if the situation that led to the irregularity is resolved. For example, one who has committed an act of schism is irregular for orders by that act. Should that person be fully reconciled to the communion of the Catholic Church, he would remain irregular for reception or exercise of orders. The same is true of vasectomy: if a vasectomy constitutes grave mutilation, and therefore an irregularity for orders, having the vasectomy reversed does not remove the irregularity. Neither does celibacy; although a celibate man is unaffected by his procreative capacity, the state of celibacy does not remove the irregularity incurred through an act of mutilation for sterility. Therefore, even those who are celibate, or have had their vasectomies reversed, must receive a dispensation prior to the reception of orders.

A prudent principle regarding dispensations from irregularities or impediments to orders is that the ordinary ought not to dispense from an impediment or an irregularity unless the person in question has withdrawn from his contumacious situation or expressed regret for his action, and has expressed acquiescence to magisterial teaching on the subject at hand. Therefore, before providing a dispensation from the irregularity incurred from a vasectomy, the ordinary or his delegate ought to discuss with the candidate the circumstances under which the vasectomy took place, the man's present perspective on the issue, and his understanding of magisterial teaching on the issue. It does not seem necessary that the candidate express his regret in a written document, but the ordinary should be satisfied that the candidate understand the gravity and the immorality of direct sterilization.

It does not seem appropriate that the ordinary require a candidate for orders to have a vasectomy reversed before being dispensed. Germain Grisez, treating the subject of sterilization in *Living a Christian Life,* notes that a man who has undergone a vasectomy and is later penitent is obliged neither to have the procedure reversed nor to abstain from ordinary conjugal relations.[6] Such a man should be careful that his sterility does not lead to a contraceptive mentality, but this issue is best discussed pastorally between the ordinary and the candidate.

The ordinary should also be attentive to scandal. If the candidate has publicly or prominently boasted of his sterility, or extolled the virtues of a sterile marriage, he might not be an appropriate candidate for a dispensation. Of course, public statements to the contrary might mitigate the scandal, so the ordinary should consider the ways in which potential scandal might be resolved.

Finally, the ordinary should be attentive to the candidate's right to his reputation, recognized in canon 220. The ordinary need not call attention to the man's irregularity, and a pastoral investigation of the situation should be undertaken with care for discretion. Should the ordinary determine not to dispense the candidate, he should afford him the opportunity to withdraw from formation, rather than publicly dismissing him. The ordinary might also afford the candidate the opportunity to continue in ecclesiastical service as he deems appropriate.

It seems clear that a vasectomy, a direct exercise of sterilization, constitutes an act of grave mutilation, and that undergoing such a procedure might lead to incurring an irregularity for orders. However, this does not mean that a man who has undergone such a procedure might not be an otherwise qualified candidate for orders. Although the ordinary should give special attention to the issues the presence of a vasectomy raises, in consideration of canon 1052, §3, if a man is otherwise qualified for ministry, the ordinary should consider the appropriateness of a dispensation when warranted. A simple decree properly prepared would suffice to remedy his legal situation.

James-Daniel Flynn, J.C.L.

---

[6] Germain Grisez, *Living a Christian Life* (Quincy, IL: Franciscan Press, 1993), 544-545.

CANON 1067

REQUIRING A FULL COURSE OF NATURAL FAMILY PLANNING AS A PRECONDITION FOR THE CELEBRATION OF MARRIAGE IN THE CATHOLIC CHURCH[1]

Can a course in a method of Natural Family Planning (NFP) be required as a precondition for the celebration of marriage in the Catholic Church?

OPINION

There is some confusion and genuine tension about what can be required of couples preparing for the celebration of marriage in the Catholic Church. The pastoral care for those preparing for marriage is the responsibility of the local bishop and his pastors. Each bishop is to ensure that marriage preparation efforts are coordinated and well planned (c. 1064). Without question, a bishop can make NFP a component of marriage preparation.[2] Strictly speaking however, a bishop cannot make participation in a course in NFP a *precondition* for the celebration of marriage in the Catholic Church.[3] It is beyond his competence.[4] The specific requirements for marriage are limited by divine, natural, and universal ecclesiastical law.

Those who develop programs for the engaged in the Church, both ordained and lay, have a framework in canon law to shape their efforts. Marriage is an original blessing of God to His creation not lost through original sin. Couples, therefore, have a natural right to enter into marriage. If a couple is free to enter into marriage and no diriment impediment exists, they cannot be prevented from exercising their natural right to marry. Thus, all persons who are not prohibited by divine or universal ecclesiastical law can contract marriage (c.

---

[1] This opinion appeared as an Appendix in the September 2008 Report of the Natural Family Planning Program of the United States Conference of Catholic Bishops (USCCB) entitled, "Requiring a Full Course of Natural Family Planning Instruction in Marriage Preparation." It is reprinted here with the permission of the USCCB Secretariat of Laity, Marriage, Family Life, and Youth. The full report may be found on the Secretariat's website at http://www.usccb.org/prolife/issues/nfp/report_requiring_% 20NFP_%2008.pdf.

[2] See c. 1063: "Pastors of souls are obliged to take care that their ecclesiastical community offers the Christian faithful the assistance by which the matrimonial state is preserved in a Christian spirit and advances in perfection...." See also c. 843, §2: "Pastors of souls and other members of the Christian faithful, according to their respective ecclesiastical function, have the duty to take care that those who seek the sacraments are prepared to receive them by proper evangelization and catechetical instruction, attentive to the norms issued by competent authority."

[3] See c. 843, §1: "Sacred ministers cannot deny the sacraments to those who seek them at appropriate times, are properly disposed, and are not prohibited by law from receiving them."

[4] Canon 838, §4: "Within the limits of his competence, it pertains to the diocesan bishop in the Church entrusted to him to issue liturgical norms which bind everyone."

1058). Regarding the requisite knowledge for marriage, the law of the Church presumes that individuals have sufficient knowledge about the nature of marriage after puberty to enter into marriage validly (c. 1096, §§1-2).

In keeping with canon 1067, the United States Conference of Catholic Bishops (USCCB) issued complementary norms, dated October 20, 2000, for marriage within the dioceses of the United States of America. The first section of the complementary norms requires marriage preparation. But the norm does not specify the content of the "appropriate education and pastoral preparation."[5] It is left up to each diocesan bishop to develop local policies or norms for marriage preparation under such headings as *The Pastoral Care to the Engaged, Diocesan Marriage Preparation Guidelines*, or *Diocesan Marriage Preparation Policies*.[6]

As the Second Vatican Council Fathers noted in *Gaudium et spes*, no. 47, much of the Western world is faced with the plague of divorce. Pope John Paul II noted that "More than ever necessary in our time is preparation of young people for marriage and family life."[7] Given the unprecedented divorce rates of the last fifty years, the challenge for bishops and pastors has been to enhance where possible the minimal requirements of the law without impeding the exercise of a couple's natural right to marry.

The Catholic Church has been at the forefront of efforts to prepare couples for marriage. Programs and practices, such as marital readiness inventories, extended periods of engagement for marriage preparation, retreat weekends, Pre-Cana days, counseling, and Evenings for the Engaged, are all elements of genuine pastoral "assistance" to the engaged.

The *Code of Canon Law* states very clearly that pastors of souls are required to offer assistance to couples preparing for marriage.[8] The "offer" of assistance, however construed or well intentioned, cannot be turned into rigid requirements for marriage (e.g., "In this diocese/parish, everyone has to take a full course in NFP and attend an Engaged Encounter Weekend to get married. No exceptions."). Ideally, engaged couples will want to make use of all of the

---

[5] See USCCB, Complementary Norms to Canon 1067, October 20, 2000, no. 1: "The couple should receive appropriate education and pastoral preparation through participation in a marriage preparation program approved by the diocesan bishop." The complete norms are posted on the USCCB's website at http://www.usccb.org/norms/1067.htm.

[6] The USCCB National Family Planning Program, 2007 *Profile*, found that ninety-eight percent of dioceses in the United States have marriage preparation guidelines.

[7] Pope John Paul II, Apostolic Exhortation, "On the Role of the Christian Family in the Modern World," *Familiaris consortio*, November 22, 1981, no. 66.

[8] See c. 1063. See also c. 843, §2.

gifts of wisdom and experience the Church offers them before marriage, especially NFP.

The question of whether or not to mandate NFP is merely the tip of the iceberg of a much larger question: How can the Church be more effective in fulfilling its mission of preparing people for marriage and family life, especially people who have been immersed in a contraceptive and hedonistic culture? Dioceses must look at all of the opportunities available to the Church to form the faithful in a Christo-centric vision of marriage and family, e.g., religious education, youth formation, family life, and education in human sexuality, etc. [9] Only when couples understand this broader context of the spousal vocation will they have the knowledge, wisdom, and inspiration to answer the "call to celebrate God's vision of human sexuality."[10]

Rev. Robert R. Cannon, J.C.L.

---

[9] See Fintan Gavin, *Pastoral Care in Marriage Preparation (Can. 1063). History, Analysis of the Norm and Its Implementation by Some Particular Churches* (Rome: Editrice Pontificia Università Gregoriana, 2004).

[10] USCCB, Committee for Pro-Life Activities, *Human Sexuality from God's Perspective*, July 25, 1993.

CANON 1108

CONVALIDATION WITH NO WITNESSES PRESENT

The vicar general officiated at a convalidation with only three people present: himself and the man and woman who exchanged consent. There were no witnesses. When the vicar general was questioned about this, he said that he had dispensed from the requirement of the witnesses and that, in any case, Ecclesia supplet. Is it possible for the bishop or his vicar general to dispense from the two witnesses required for canonical form, and is this a valid marriage?

OPINION

The presence of two witnesses is an essential element of the canonical form (c. 1108, §1). It is thus a requirement of constitutive law, which may not be dispensed (c. 86). The canonical form itself may be dispensed, and the law itself permits some exceptions to it, but there can be no observance of the canonical form without two witnesses. The dispensing power of the diocesan bishop from universal disciplinary laws (c. 87, §1) is not applicable here. Thus, the dispensation (whether given by the vicar general or the bishop) can only be from the canonical form itself, not from the two witnesses. The question must therefore be redirected as to whether this was a valid dispensation from canonical form.

There are four situations foreseen in the law when the local ordinary may dispense from canonical form: (1) In a mixed marriage, if grave difficulties hinder the observance of the canonical form by the Catholic party (c. 1127, §2). When both parties are Catholic, the dispensation from canonical form is normally reserved to the Apostolic See[1]; (2) when one of the parties had defected from the Catholic faith and converted to another non-Catholic confession.[2] Also in this situation, grave difficulties must stand in the way of the observance of the canonical form[3]; (3) when either party to the marriage is

---

[1]Pontifical Commission for the Authentic Interpretation of the Code of Canon Law, Reply, May 14, 1985, *Acta Apostolicae Sedis* 77 (1985) 771; English translation in *Canon Law Digest* 11:14.

[2] Pontifical Council for the Interpretation of the Decrees of the Second Vatican Council, Reply, February 11, 1972, *Acta Apostolicae Sedis* 64 (1972) 397; English translation in *Canon Law Digest* 7:750.

[3] See Pope Paul VI, Apostolic Letter *motu proprio*, *Matrimonia mixta*, March 31, 1970, *Acta Apostolicae Sedis* 62 (1970) 257-263, no. 9; English translation in *Canon Law Digest* 7:716. The

in danger of death (*urgente mortis periculo*). In that case, the local ordinary may dispense not only from the canonical form but from every impediment of ecclesiastical law, whether public or occult, except the impediment arising from the sacred order of the presbyterate (c. 1079, §1); and (4) in the marriage of two Catholics, if recourse to the Holy See is difficult and, at the same time, there is danger of grave harm in delay, provided that it concerns a dispensation which the Holy See is accustomed to grant under the same circumstances (c. 87, §2).

For a valid dispensation, there must be a just and reasonable cause, and the dispensing authority must take into account the circumstances of the case and the importance of the law being dispensed (c. 90, §1). Thus, even if this case involved one of the four exceptions when the local ordinary could dispense, the dispensation would have been invalid without a just and reasonable cause in consideration of the circumstances of the case and the gravity of the law.

In reference to the remark "*Ecclesia supplet*," it is evident that canon 144 is irrelevant to the case. It is applicable only to the supply of the faculty to assist at marriage, which the vicar general has in virtue of his office (c. 1108, §1), not to the requirement of having two witnesses. In sum, this attempted convalidation in all likelihood was invalid, either because the parties were not eligible to be dispensed from canonical form, or because the motive and circumstances did not justify it. If so, it may be advisable to seek a radical sanation (c. 1161, §1).

John M. Huels, J.C.D.

---

authentic interpretation cited in note 2 must be read in conjunction with this *motu proprio*, which was the basis for the interpretation.

CANON 1116, §1, 2°

CELEBRATION OF THE EXTRAORDINARY FORM OF MARRIAGE OUTSIDE THE DANGER OF DEATH

A widow and widower in my parish wish to marry in the Church. Both are good Catholics. Canonically there is no problem, both are free to marry, but if they obtain a marriage license and marry, the woman, who is relatively young, will lose the sizable military pension from her deceased husband. If a priest or deacon would officiate at their marriage without a marriage license, in our state he would commit a class B misdemeanor and would be subject to a fine and imprisonment. Is there a solution for their problem?

OPINION

This is not a merely theoretical problem for many couples. On the one hand, they would not suffer the important financial loss of a pension if they would simply live together in sin—and the state would do nothing; today civil law could not care less. On the other hand, this would be contrary to their conscience. Undocumented immigrants face a similar problem. If they apply for a marriage license, they fear that the danger of deportation is even greater.

A somewhat analogous situation existed in Germany, as in many other countries, which required a civil marriage before a state official, prior to a Church marriage. Germany modified its law governing civil marriages and the Episcopal Conference of Germany enacted new norms, which were promulgated by the diocesan bishops in their dioceses:

> The prohibition of a Church marriage without a prior civil marriage is not applicable according to the amendment of the law of personal rights (*Personenstandrechts* [of Germany]) on January 1, 2009. From such a Church marriage no rights are conferred in the civil law. Wherefore it is fitting that for the Church that a civil marriage be contracted. In this way the rights of the faithful will be assured.[1]

Taking into account this change in German law, the Episcopal Conference of Germany enacted norms for the celebration of Church marriages without a prior civil marriage. A *nihil obstat* must be obtained for a Church marriage

---

[1] Deutsche Bischofskonferenz, "Nr. 199, Ordnung für kirchliche Trauungen bei fehlender Ziviletheschließung," in *Kirchliches Amtsblatt für Diözese Fulda* XV (December 5, 2008), 133; trans. William H. Woestman, O.M.I.

without a previous civil marriage. Prior to the granting of a *nihil obstat*, the bride and groom have to sign a declaration in which they acknowledge that they had been instructed that they will not be considered to be married according to the law of the State; have no legal claim for mutual maintenance; do not enjoy any legal marriage inheritance rights; are not permitted to use a common surname; cannot receive from the marriage any derivative pension rights, e.g., a widow's pension or annuity; are treated according to tax laws as not married; unlike those married civilly, they do not have in court an exemption from giving testimony; it also means that the children that they may have together will be considered in civil law as children of unmarried parents. In a declaration the couple has to affirm that they will fulfill all the duties flowing from a Church marriage, including the material welfare of one's spouse and children. The couple must also give the grounds why they do not want a civil marriage. Only then will the local ordinary grant a *nihil obstat* for the Church celebration of the marriage.

Although the reasons for seeking a Church marriage in the United States without a marriage license may be similar to the grounds for not having a civil marriage in Germany, there is a major difference. In Germany, the pastor or other authorized priest or deacon officiates at the Church marriage as he would for any other marriage. In the United States, the priest or deacon cannot legally officiate at a marriage without a marriage license.

Is there another way out of this dilemma? According to canon 1116:

> §1. If a person competent to assist according to the norm of law cannot be present or approached without grave inconvenience, those who intend to enter into a true marriage can contract it validly and licitly before [two] witnesses only:
>
> 2° outside the danger of death provided that it is prudently foreseen that the situation will continue for a month.

It seems that in the abovementioned case all of the provisions exist for contracting marriage according to the extraordinary form, i.e., in the situation, no priest or deacon will be available for a month, and there is a grave inconvenience. When this is the case, the couple can marry validly and licitly. No intervention of a bishop, priest, or deacon is necessary. The marriage contracted in this way is a Catholic marriage on par with any marriage celebrated before a duly authorized priest or deacon and two witnesses.

I hear immediately the cry: "Wait a minute! With the fulfillment of all the provisions for preparation for marriage, pre-nuptial investigation, etc. we still have many invalid marriages. This will only make matters worse."

First of all, if a couple has the right according to the Code to marry using the extraordinary form, no bishop or pastor has the authority to forbid them to do so.

They do not have to ask anyone for a *nihil obstat* or permission. It seems that pastoral solicitude demands that a couple must be informed of their right to marry using the extraordinary form to celebrate the sacrament whenever the necessary conditions are verified. The people have the right to know the law, and it should be explained to them—the contrary attitude is most paternalistic. At the same time, pastoral provisions should be taken to assure, insofar as possible, that they are properly prepared for marriage with the necessary precautions taken as for marriages celebrated using the ordinary form.

Unlike the ordinary form which requires that the one officiating "asks for the manifestation of the consent ... and receives it in the name of the Church" (c. 1108, §2), it is sufficient for the couple to manifest their marital consent, i.e., their intention of contracting marriage here and now, before two witnesses. Lest there be even the appearance of violating civil law, it is advisable that a priest or deacon not be present for the actual exchange of the marriage consent. In this way, it is clear that he is not officiating at a marriage celebrated without a license.

The marriage according to the extraordinary form has all the effects, rights, and obligations of natural and ecclesiastical law, even if it is not recognized by the State. If both persons are baptized, it is a sacramental marriage. If there is an impediment to their marrying that can be dispensed, the diocesan bishop or his delegate can grant a dispensation according to the norms of the Code.

The prescriptions of canon 1121 for the registration of the marriage must be followed. Although a priest or deacon could not officiate at the marriage because of a "grave inconvenience," nothing impedes having a nuptial Mass and the conferral of the nuptial blessing some time—even immediately—after the celebration of the marriage. According to the *Code of Canons of the Eastern Catholic Churches*, which has the same norms for the extraordinary form of marriage as the Code for the Latin Church, the couple should receive the nuptial blessing as soon as possible:

> Can. 832 §3. If a marriage was celebrated in the presence only of witnesses, the spouses shall not neglect to receive the blessing of the marriage from a priest as soon as possible.

Rev. William H. Woestman, O.M.I., J.C.D.

Canon 1160

Defective Convalidation

A parishioner recently contacted me to begin a process for the declaration of nullity of his former marriage. He and his former spouse had been married civilly, but they later convalidated their marriage in the Catholic Church. Is it advisable to introduce the man's petition on the ground of "defective convalidation" since, from what he tells me, the wife believed the civil marriage made the couple husband and wife and the Church ceremony was merely a "blessing" on their marriage?

Opinion

The answer to this question is assisted by the recent guidance of the Supreme Tribunal of the Apostolic Signatura, both in a decree[1] issued November 23, 2005, and in a letter[2] dated December 19, 2007, to a cardinal-archbishop in the United States of America. The decree was issued in response to a plea from the defender of the bond of the Roman Rota who had been concerned that a rotal decision on "defective convalidation" had not appropriately applied the marriage canons to a marriage celebrated after its parties had entered a "civil union" without regard for canonical form. The letter was issued to assist tribunals in accurately and justly applying the same laws in the same situation.

The decree and letter provide invaluable insights into the proper canonical understanding of the "marriage" of a Catholic which was celebrated without regard for canonical form (i.e., the required form had not been dispensed [c. 1127, §2], the Catholic had not defected from the Church by a formal act [c. 1117], the situation in which to employ extraordinary form did not exist [c. 1116], and the Catholic did not marry a non-Catholic of an Eastern rite in the presence of a sacred minister and in observance of other legal requirements

---

[1] Supreme Tribunal of the Apostolic Signatura, Decree, Prot. No. 34622/03 CG, November 23, 2005, in Periodica 26 (2007) 283-288.

[2] Supreme Tribunal of the Apostolic Signatura, Letter, Prot. No. 1034/07 SAT, 185/07 ES, December 19 2007, in *Roman Replies and CLSA Advisory Opinions 2008*, eds. Joseph J. Koury and Siobhan M. Verbeek (Washington, DC: Canon Law Society of America, 2008), 54-56. See also Wojciech Kowal, O.M.I. and William H. Woestman, O.M.I., *Special Marriage Cases and Procedures*, 4th rev. ed. (Ottawa: Faculty of Canon Law Saint Paul University, 2008), 231-233. Apparently, moderators of several tribunals in the United States received similar letters.

where Catholic form is required only for liceity [c. 1127, §2]). The Apostolic Signatura's guidance assists both in preparing Catholics who are in a union that was entered into without regard for canonical form for marriage, and in the evaluation of their subsequent Catholic marriage should a petition for its nullity be presented to a tribunal.

As will become evident in the following, the juridic system of the Catholic Church gives no recognition to the "marriage" of a Catholic who had completely disregarded canonical form. Such is neither a "null marriage" nor an "invalid marriage." It is simply no "marriage."[3] Therefore, for the sake of precision reflecting Church law, we will term such a relationship a "civil union."

Guidance from the Decree and the Letter

The following conclusions are drawn from a careful reading of both the decree and the letter issued by the Apostolic Signatura:

1. Every marriage celebrated in canonical form is presumed valid until the contrary is proven (c. 1060). One cannot presume that the parties in a "civil union" do not enter a valid marriage when subsequently exchanging consent *coram Ecclesiam*.
2. "The internal consent of the mind is presumed to conform to the words or signs used in celebrating the marriage" (c. 1101, §1). One cannot presume that the parties in a "civil union" simulate when subsequently exchanging consent in canonical form.

---

[3] Various commentators have given various descriptions to what we are terming a "civil union." Arturo Jemolo says it is not merely "null by defect of form" but is simply "non-existent." See A. Jemolo, *Il matrimonio nel diritto canonico* (Milan: F. Vallardi, 1941), 307, no. 165. Francisco Wernz and Petrus Vidal say it is "legal and public concubinage." See F. Wernz and P. Vidal, *Ius canonicum ad Codicis normam exactum*, 3rd ed. (Rome: Apud Aedes Universitatis Gregorianae, 1946), V:751, no. 594. Eduardus Regatillo calls it "mere concubinage." See E. Regatillo, *Ius Sacramentarium*, 4th ed. (Santander: Sal Terrae, 1964), 598-599, no. 1049. Urbano Navarette says it simply "is not a marriage." See U. Navarette, "Ecclesia sanat in radice matrimonia initia cum impedimento iuris divini," *Periodica* 52 (1963) 376.
Further, the non-existence of a "civil union" as a marriage is evident from the August 7, 1984 authentic interpretation of the Pontifical Commission for the Authentic Interpretation of the Code of Canon Law which explains that the determination of the free status to marry of a person who had been in an earlier "civil union" rests with the pastor conducting the prenuptial investigation of the party. See *Acta Apostolicae Sedis* 76 (1984) 747; English translation in *Canon Law Digest* 11:351. The "documentary process" outlined in cc. 1686-1688 concerns only marriages with a "defect of form" (not civil unions entered with a total "lack of form"). The Code has no judicial process for "lack of form" situations since the Church does not recognize their existence in its juridic system. The universal law does not expect that the tribunal will be involved in investigating unions begun with a "lack of form."

3. Canon 1160 refers to the convalidation of a marriage invalid due to a "defect of form." It applies when a couple observed canonical form when initiating their marriage, but something defective in the form prevented the marriage from being valid (e.g., the *assistens* lacked jurisdiction, the required two witnesses were not present, the *assistens* did not ask for and receive consent in the name of the Church: see cc. 1108; 1112, §2). The marriage is "null" because the attempted canonical form was somehow defective. Catholics who enter a "civil union" begin their relationship with a total "lack of form," not with a "defect" in the attempted canonical form. Canon 1160 cannot be applied when they seek to regularize their relationship in the Church.
4. It is not proper to speak of a "renewal of consent" when partners in a "civil union" celebrate marriage in canonical form. Canon 1157, which mentions the "renewal of consent," concerns only the convalidation of a marriage invalid due to a diriment impediment. Parties to a "civil union," when entering marriage in canonical form, are simply giving consent to marriage. They are not renewing the consent they had expressed when entering their "civil union."
5. When parties in a "civil union" approach the Church to exchange consent, it must be presumed that they somehow understand that the "civil union" is not a true marriage and, therefore, until the contrary is proven, it must be presumed that they elicit matrimonial consent *coram Ecclesiam*. The very fact that the couple approaches the Church for a marriage in canonical form indicates that they somehow know their "civil union" is not a marriage.
6. It is sufficient for the validity of the exchange of consent *coram Ecclesiam* that the parties understand vaguely that the "civil union" lacked an essential element considered significant by the Catholic Church–i.e., the canonical form.
7. This sufficient and vague understanding of the "civil union" does not demand that the parties know how to explain its nonexistence as a marriage in a technical-canonical manner.
8. On the emotional level, the parties may continue to attribute some value (e.g., existential or in civil law) to the "civil union" (for example, by celebrating its anniversary). Attributing such value to the "civil union" does not indicate that true matrimonial consent is not exchanged *coram Ecclesiam*.

9. The parties are not required to explain in technical-canonical language what happens at the exchange of consent in canonical form. Even if they use canonically improper terms (e.g., "blessing") to describe it, until the contrary is proven, it is presumed that they give true consent *coram Ecclesiam* and thereby establish a true marriage. This reflects the presumed validity of marriage (c. 1060).
10. Even if a party considers the exchange of consent in canonical form to have no value, attention must be given to the discipline of canon 1100: "The knowledge or opinion of the nullity of a marriage does not necessarily exclude matrimonial consent." In other words, if a party thinks the exchange of consent *coram Ecclesiam* lacks merit, this error does not necessarily prove that the party did not exchange valid consent.
11. To prove the invalidity of the exchange of consent *coram Ecclesiam* of those in a "civil union," the customary criteria must be applied.

Application to the Preparation for Marriage of Couples in a "Civil Union"

The decree and letter of the Apostolic Signatura provide guidance to a pastor who is preparing a couple in a "civil union" for a marriage in canonical form. He will keep in mind the following:

1. He should explain, in pastorally sensitive but clear terms, that the Church does not recognize the existence of the "civil union" as a marriage because the required canonical form was disregarded.[4] Consequently, when the parties exchange consent *coram Ecclesiam*, they will be marrying *for the first time in the eyes of God*.
2. He should avoid referring to the "civil union" as a "marriage," since the Church does not give juridic recognition to that union.
3. He should avoid referring to the exchange of consent in canonical form as a "convalidation." The term "convalidation" is used in canon law only in regard to a relationship which has the semblance of a marriage but is "invalid/null" due to an impediment (cc. 1156-1158), defective consent (c. 1159) or a

[4] "Civil unions" do not have juridic existence, yet they do have *moral* relevance. In the Apostolic Exhortation, *Familiaris consortio*, Pope John Paul II distinguishes those in "civil unions" (no. 82) from those who cohabit with neither civil nor religious recognition of their relationship (no. 81). See *Acta Apostolicae Sedis* 74 (1982) 181-184.

defect in form (c. 1160). As mentioned above, a "civil union" had been entered with a "lack of form," not a "defect of form." Rather, the pastor should speak of the pending "marriage" of the partners.

4. He should avoid saying that the exchange of consent *coram Ecclesiam* will be a "blessing" of the "civil union." The exchange of consent is a juridic act whereby a valid marriage is established between the partners in a "civil union." It is not a blessing on the union. Indeed, should a partner seek only a blessing on a "civil union" and nothing more, it is likely that the object of his or her juridic act is not marriage but the blessing. As a result, after the exchange of consent the partners would have neither a marriage nor a blessing, since no marriage exists which can be blessed!
5. If, during the preparation for marriage of a couple in a "civil union," it becomes evident that one or both are personally unwilling or psychologically unable to elicit a valid exchange of consent (e.g., because the party insists that the couple is already married in the eyes of God and, therefore, their consent *coram Ecclesiam* would have something other than marriage as its object), on a case-by-case basis, the competent authority may grant the favor of a *radical sanation* of the couple's "civil union."[5]

   Radical sanation is an *extraordinary* means of rectifying an invalid marriage or a "civil union." Some may question how a "civil union," if not recognized by the Church as an "invalid/null" marriage, can be sanated radically by the same Church. The answer lies in the nature of a juridic act and a radical sanation. For a Catholic, the juridic act of marriage requires for its validity that the exchange of consent take place with regard for canonical form (see c. 124, §1).[6] If canonical form is disregarded (lacking), the juridic act simply does not exist. Nonetheless, the parties may elicit naturally sufficient matrimonial consent when they enter the "civil union." Radical sanation, which by law "entails the dispensation ... from canonical form, if it was not observed" (c. 1161, §1), requires that "the consent of each party perseveres" (c. 1163, §1).

[5] See Urbano Navarette, "A propositio del Decreto del S. T. della Segnatura Apostolica de 23 novembre 2005," *Periodica* 96 (2007) 335-336.

[6] See Augustine Mendonça, "Defective Convalidation," *CLSA Proceedings* 70 (2008) 194-195.

Therefore, if the parties elicited naturally sufficient matrimonial consent, although the consent did not result in a marriage because an element required for the validity of the juridic act of marriage was absent, their "civil union" can be radically sanated. Obviously, the decision to sanate radically a "civil union" must be made on a case-by-case basis by the competent ecclesiastical authority after it has ascertained that use of this *extraordinary* remedy is appropriate, that naturally sufficient matrimonial consent had been elicited by both parties when they entered the "civil union," and that such consent perdures.

Application to Marriage Nullity Petitions

The decree and letter of the Apostolic Signatura also provide guidance to tribunals investigating the consent exchanged *coram Ecclesiam* by parties who are already together in a "civil union." All involved in nullity petitions involving such consent will keep in mind the following:

1. The ground of nullity cannot be "defective convalidation." As mentioned above, a "civil union," since it lacks canonical form and has no semblance to a marriage, is not subject to "convalidation." (The term "defective convalidation" can be used only when investigating the defect in the convalidation of a marriage "null/invalid" because of an impediment, defective consent, or a *defect* of form.)
2. The tribunal's investigation will not make reference to a "renewal of consent" by the couple in a "civil union," as sometimes has been done. "Renewal of consent" is a term applied only to the convalidation of a marriage invalid because of an impediment (cc. 1156-1158). Indeed, when marrying *coram Ecclesiam*, partners in a "civil union" are not asked to "renew" consent; rather, they are asked to "give/elicit" consent.[7]
3. The focus of the tribunal's investigation must be the matrimonial consent exchanged *coram Ecclesiam* by the parties.[8] Therefore, the declarations of the parties and all the

---

[7] Kenneth Boccafola, when discussing the consent expressed *coram Ecclesiam* by those in a "civil union," writes: "It matters little if we call this consent *first, new* or *renewed*, provided that it is clear to all that there was an actual, effective matrimonial consent, present at the moment of the canonical celebration of marriage." See *coram* Boccafola (March 12, 1998), *RRT Dec.* 90 (1998) 232-233, no. 11; English translation approved by Boccafola. See *Studia Canonica* 34 (2000) 523.
[8] See Lynda Robitaille, "Defective Validation of Marriages Lacking Canonical Form: An Interpretation of Total Simulation," *The Jurist* 66 (2006) 436-468.

other proofs in nullity proceedings must focus on the consent elicited when establishing marriage, not when they began the "civil union." The consent of the partners to their "civil union" is not the subject of the tribunal's study, since it is not a marriage.

To investigate what happened during the "civil union" prior to the marriage is also important, of course, but it is equivalent to an investigation of the pre-marital personal and relational lives of parties who had never been in a civil union.

4. When investigating the consent *coram Ecclesiam* of partners in a "civil union," the tribunal may consider the same grounds of nullity as it does when studying *any* marriage. The grounds may focus on consensual incapacity (c. 1095), defects of the intellect (cc. 1096-1099), and defects of the will (cc. 1101-1103) present in either or both parties. Each partner must have consensual capacity and the absence of invalidating intellectual and voluntary defects at the time of the marriage. Any incapacity or invalidating defects present at the time of entering the "civil union" have no juridic consequence (except, of course, inasmuch as they may reflect issues that remain present at the time of the marriage in canonical form).

   Prudently, the tribunal may give special focus to possible total simulation by either partner in a "civil union" when the couple marries *coram Ecclesiam.*[9] Obviously, as the Apostolic Signatura rightly observes, one must presume that these partners elicit valid consent in the canonical form. Nonetheless, given the social and personal acceptance of their "civil union," the partners may be convinced it is their true marriage. Consequently, when exchanging consent in canonical form, the object of their consent may be *something other than the establishment of marriage*. They may exchange consent *coram Ecclesiam* only to achieve the Church's recognition of their "civil union," to be readmitted the sacraments, to receive the Church's "blessing" on their relationship, to please nagging family members, etc. Admittedly, any of these may be *motives* accompanying valid consent, but each may also *replace*

---

[9] See *coram* Boccafola (March 12, 1998), *RRT Dec*. 90 (1998) 234-235, no. 13; English translation approved by Boccafola. See *Studia Canonica* 34 (2000) 523-224; Lynda Robitaille, "Defective Convalidations Revisited," in *In the Service of Justice: Festschrift in Honour of Prof. Augustine Mendonça*, ed. Victor D'Souza, (Bangalore: St. Peter's Pontifical Institute, 2008), 167-190.

> marriage as the object of one's consent, particularly if the partner is convinced the couple is already married. In other words, the object of marriage consent (i.e., to establish marriage) may be excluded by a positive act of the will and replaced with something else. This is total simulation (c. 1101).

The guidance of the Apostolic Signatura provides helpful insights to what is necessary and sufficient for the valid marriage of a Catholic in a "civil union." It will assist both the pastoral preparation of couples in a "civil union" who wish to enter marriage, and the practice of tribunals that investigate the consent given by the partners in a "civil union" when they enter marriage *coram Ecclesiam*. It may require adjustments in the practical life and ministry of the Church, even in the language commonly used to describe both "civil unions" and the consent which its partners may eventually exchange in canonical form.

In answer to the question posed, the tribunal will focus on the consent of the parties exchanged *coram Ecclesiam*. The investigation will be on the consent *de praesenti* whose object must be marriage in all its aspects. The joinder of the issues must not be "defective convalidation" since this term cannot be applied when partners in a "civil union" exchange consent before the Church. The use of inaccurate terminology by the wife (e.g., blessing of their marriage) and her belief that they were already a married couple before the Church ceremony, may or may not indicate the total simulation of her consent *coram Ecclesiam*. Further, the tribunal may also investigate whether other grounds of nullity may pertain, since when couples in a "civil union" exchange consent in canonical form, the object of their consent is necessarily the marriage in all its aspects. A number of factors may invalidate this matrimonial consent: i.e., human incapacity, defects of the intellect, or defects of the will.

Rev. Msgr. John A. Renken, J.C.D.

CANON 1248, §1

ATTENDANCE AT MASSES CELEBRATED BY PRIESTS OF THE SOCIETY OF ST. PIUS X

Now that the excommunications of the four bishops ordained by Archbishop Marcel Lefebvre have been remitted, are the faithful free to attend Masses celebrated by priests of the Society of St. Pius X? Will this fulfill the Sunday Mass obligation?

OPINION

The topic of fulfilling the Sunday Mass obligation in so-called "traditionalist" churches has been addressed in two earlier contradictory advisory opinions.[1] New legislation and recent clarifications from the Holy See necessitate a reexamination of this issue.

Remission of Excommunication

In response to repeated requests from the superior general of the Society of St. Pius X (SSPX), the excommunications of the four bishops illicitly consecrated by Archbishop Marcel Lefebvre were remitted on January 21, 2009.[2] The decree noted that this remission occurred out of "paternal compassion" and to facilitate dialogue between the SSPX and the Holy See. A note of the Secretariat of State made the following important clarification:

> The remission of the excommunication has freed the four bishops from a serious canonical penalty, but it has not changed the juridical position of the Society of St. Pius X, which presently does not enjoy any canonical recognition by the Catholic Church. The four bishops, even though they have been released from excommunication, have no canonical function in the church and do not licitly exercise a ministry within it.[3]

---

[1] See James J. Cuneo and James H. Provost, "Fulfilling the Sunday Mass Obligation in a Traditionalist Church," *CLSA Advisory Opinions 1984-1993*, ed. Patrick J. Cogan, S.A. (Washington, DC: Canon Law Society of America, 1995), 400-403 and 403-407 respectively.

[2] Congregation for Bishops, Decree Remitting the Excommunication of Bishops Consecrated by Lefebvre, January 21, 2009, *L'Osservatore Romano*, vol. 149, no. 20 (January 25, 2009), 1; English translation in *Origins* 38 (2009) 533-534.

[3] Secretariat of State, Note Concerning the Remitting of Excommunication of SSPX Bishops, February 4, 2009, *L'Osservatore Romano*, vol. 149, no. 29 (February 5, 2009), 1; English translation in *Origins* 38 (2009) 570.

In an unusual move, Pope Benedict XVI himself confronted this issue once more in a letter addressed to all bishops:

> The remission of the excommunication was a measure taken in the field of ecclesiastical discipline: The individuals were freed from the burden of conscience constituted by the most serious of ecclesiastical penalties.
>
> This disciplinary level needs to be distinguished from the doctrinal level. The fact that the Society of St. Pius X does not possess a canonical status in the church is not, in the end, based on disciplinary but on doctrinal reasons. As long as the society does not have a canonical status in the church, its ministers do not exercise legitimate ministries in the church. There needs to be a distinction, then, between the disciplinary level, which deals with individuals as such, and the doctrinal level, at which ministry and institution are involved. In order to make this clear once again: Until the doctrinal questions are clarified, the society has no canonical status in the church, and its ministers—even though they have been freed of the ecclesiastical penalty—do not legitimately exercise any ministry in the church.[4]

Priests and deacons of the SSPX "do not legitimately exercise ministry in the Church" because they remain suspended *ipso facto* from the order received in virtue of canon 1383, that is, in violation of canon 1015, requiring every candidate to sacred orders to be ordained by his proper bishop or with legitimate dimissorial letters from him. The remission of excommunication of the four bishops ordained by Archbishop Lefebvre remains just that, a remission of a serious ecclesiastical penalty. This remission does not alter or enhance the juridic status of the SSPX or the ministry exercised by those clerics adhering to this movement.

Adherence to Schism

The 1983 *Code of Canon Law* defines schism as "the refusal of submission to the Supreme Pontiff or of communion with the members of the Church subject to him" (c. 751). Consequently, a schismatic incurs a *latae sententiae* excommunication (c. 1364, §1). The Apostolic Letter *motu proprio Ecclesia Dei*, following the declared excommunication of Archbishop Lefebvre and

---

[4] Pope Benedict XVI, Letter to Bishops on the Lifting of the Excommunication of Lefebvrite Bishops, March 10, 2009, in *Origins* 38 (2009), 647.

those he ordained, recalled that "everyone should be aware that formal adherence to the schism is a grave offence against God and carries the penalty of excommunication decreed by the Church's law" (no. 5).[5] "Formal adherence" involves two complementary elements:

a) One is by its nature internal, consisting in sharing freely and consciously in the substance of the schism, that is in the decision by the followers of Archbishop Lefebvre that one makes that choice over obedience to the pope–at the root of this attitude there will ordinarily be positions contrary to the Church's magisterium;
b) The other is by its nature external, consisting in the exteriorization of this choice, the most evident sign of this will be the exclusive participation in Lefebvrite "ecclesial" acts, without taking part in the acts of the Catholic Church. This is, however, a sign that is not univocal, since there is the possibility that some members of the faithful participate in the liturgical functions of the followers of Lefebvre without, however, sharing in their schismatic spirit (no. 5).[6]

The same letter states that, in the case of SSPX deacons and priests, "it seems certain that their ministerial activity within the schismatic movement is a very clear sign of the fact that the two requirements mentioned above (no. 5) are present and that there is therefore a formal adherence" (no. 6). Consequently, it appears that the bishops, priests and deacons of the SSPX, and members of the faithful who formally adhere to it, remain subject to the censure of excommunication *latae sententiae* (c. 1331, §1). This, however, has never been formally declared by the Holy See. Occasional participation in the liturgical acts or activities of the SSPX does not necessarily constitute formal adherence to schism (no. 7).

Sunday Mass Obligation

"On Sundays and other holy days of obligation, the faithful are obliged to participate in the Mass" (c. 1247). According to canon 1248, §1: "The person

---

[5] Pope John Paul II, Apostolic Letter motu proprio Ecclesia Dei, July 2, 1988, *Acta Apostolicae Sedis* 80 (1988) 1495-1498; English translation in *Canon Law Digest* 12:805-808.

[6] Pontifical Council for the Interpretation of Legislative Texts, Note concerning the excommunication incurred because of schism by followers of Lefebvre, August 24, 1996, in *Communicationes* 29 (1997) 241-243; English translation in William H. Woestman, O.M.I., *Ecclesiastical Sanctions and the Penal Process*, 2nd rev. ed. (Ottawa: Faculty of Canon Law, Saint Paul University, 2003), 201-203.

who assists at a Mass celebrated anywhere in a Catholic rite either on the feast day itself or in the evening of the preceding day satisfies the obligation of participating in the Mass." The term "Catholic rite" used in canon 1248 is somewhat ambiguous, reflecting the fact that "rite" is used imprecisely throughout the Code. It can refer either to "ritual churches" or to the various liturgical rituals contained in the duly promulgated liturgical books.

Can a Mass celebrated by a priest of the SSPX fulfill this obligation? A successful resolution depends on how one interprets "Catholic rite."

On the one hand, one may interpret "Catholic rite" as a "ritual Church" or, more correctly, as a Church *sui iuris*.[7] The SSPX is a schismatic movement of the Latin Church and, evidently, does not constitute a Church *sui iuris*. Its buildings and institutions are not legitimately designated as places of worship by the competent ecclesiastical authority. In fact, the SSPX–despite its protests–possesses no juridic personality in the Church. Participation at Mass is an external expression of ecclesial communion. This is precisely why intercommunion (*communicatio in sacris*) with baptized non-Catholics is only permitted under certain conditions (see c. 844). Clerics of the SSPX are not in full communion with the Catholic Church as they refuse to submit to the authority legitimately exercised by the Roman Pontiff and the college of bishops (see c. 205). Consequently, one cannot fulfill the Sunday obligation at Masses celebrated by priests who adhere to a schismatic movement, who exercise no official ministry in the Church, and who refuse to submit to legitimate ecclesiastical governance. As James Provost argues, "[I]t does not make sense to speak of Catholics fulfilling an obligation they have within the Catholic communion by participating at Mass outside that communion."[8]

On the other hand, one may interpret "Catholic rite" as a Mass celebrated according to an approved Catholic ritual. After the promulgation of the revised *Missale Romanum* in 1970, use of the earlier Missal was permitted in only exceptional circumstances and by means of an indult. Now, in accordance with the July 2007 Apostolic Letter *motu proprio Summorum Pontificum*, use of the earlier Missal constitutes the "extraordinary form" of the "one Roman rite."

---

[7] *The Code of Canons of the Eastern Churches* (CCEO) provides greater precision and specifies that "A rite is the liturgical, theological, spiritual and disciplinary patrimony, culture and circumstances of the history of a distinct people, by which its own manner of living the faith is manifested in each Church sui iuris" (c. 28, §1). A "rite," therefore, is not a Church *sui iuris*, but the patrimony expressed therein.

[8] James H. Provost, "Fulfilling the Sunday Mass Obligation in a Traditionalist Church," *CLSA Advisory Opinions 1984-1993*, ed. Patrick J. Cogan, S.A. (Washington, DC: Canon Law Society of America, 1995), 406.

One may reasonably argue that there is no question that Masses celebrated according to the 1962 *editio typica* of the *Missale Romanum* constitute a "Catholic rite." Although Masses celebrated by priests of the SSPX may constitute a "Catholic rite," and the faithful assisting may fulfill their obligation according to canon 1248, §1, these Masses are illicitly celebrated.

To add further support to this position, one should note the legislative history of this canon. Earlier drafts of canon 1248 had qualified the fulfillment of this obligation to Masses that were "legitimately celebrated." The commission acknowledged that the causes of illegitimacy often reside with the sacred minister and the Christian faithful ought not to be punished for such a fault of the sacred minister.[9] Consequently, one can argue that the Christian faithful can fulfill the Sunday obligation even at Masses illegitimately celebrated by a sacred minister. For example, if a Mass was celebrated by a priest irregular for the exercise of orders as a result of positively cooperating in procuring a completed abortion (c. 1044, §1, 3°), or by a suspended priest who had attempted marriage (c. 1394, §1), the faithful assisting would still fulfill their Sunday obligation. In the case of a Mass celebrated by a priest of the SSPX, the illegitimacy of such a Mass clearly resides with the priest. The faithful are not to be punished by the fault of the sacred minister and, therefore, may reasonably fulfill the obligation of canon 1248, §1 in such cases.[10]

There may well be reasonable disagreement over which of the two arguments is the stronger. Both arguments present several difficulties. If one

---

[9] The draft canon read as follows: "Legi de Missae participando satisfacit qui Missae assistit ubicumque legitime celebratur ritu catholico." For the discussion of the Pontifical Commission for the Revision of the Code, see *Communicationes* 12 (1980) 361-362.

[10] In a recent interview, Cardinal Darío Castrillón Hoyos, President of the Pontifical Commission *Ecclesia Dei*, stated the following concerning clerics of the SSPX: "The Masses they celebrate are undoubtedly valid but not licit; thus, participation is not advised except on Sundays when there are no other alternatives" (G. Biccini, "A Two-fold use of the one Roman Rite," in *L'Osservatore Romano*, Weekly English Edition, April 9, 2008, 4). It is not entirely clear from this statement whether Castrillón Hoyos believes the faithful, under these circumstances, fulfill the obligation of c. 1248, §1, or whether the law dispenses from this obligation due to the impossibility of assisting at a Mass licitly celebrated (c. 1248, §2). Periodically, private replies from the Pontifical Commission *Ecclesia Dei* are posted online. One such reply, dated January 18, 2003, indicates that in the "strict sense" the obligation of c. 1248, §1 can be fulfilled at Masses celebrated by priests of the SSPX. Nevertheless, in this and other replies, *Ecclesia Dei* strongly discourages the faithful from attending these Masses on a habitual basis for fear it will lead to a schismatic mentality. Regardless of the content, these responses are private replies and make no pretense of being authentic interpretations, a competency not exercised by the Pontifical Commission *Ecclesia Dei*. Consequently, these private replies have no force of law. See, for example, http://www.ewtn.com/library/CURIA/CEDSSPX.HTM and http://www.ewtn.com/library/CURIA/CEDSSPX2.HTM [accessed June 2009].

affirms that the obligation can be fulfilled at Masses celebrated by SSPX priests, the obligation to maintain communion with the Church (c. 209, §1) is compromised. Full communion with the Catholic Church consists of a threefold expression, namely, through the bonds of the profession of faith, the sacraments and ecclesiastical governance (c. 205). Although attendance, even frequent attendance, at these Masses may not constitute formal adherence to schism, the faithful's external actions suggest a refusal to submit to the authority legitimately exercised by the Roman Pontiff who, by means of *Summorum Pontificum*, has attempted to satisfy the requests of "traditionalists" by generously permitting wider use of earlier liturgical forms.

Similarly, if one affirms that the obligation cannot be fulfilled at Masses celebrated by priests of the SSPX, one is at odds with the legislative history of canon 1248. The 1983 Code no longer specifies the place where the Mass obligation can be fulfilled (as did *CIC*/17, c. 1249). Canon 1248, §1 states that the obligation can be fulfilled in a Catholic rite celebrated "anywhere" (*ubicumque*). As well, changes introduced into canon 1248, before its official promulgation, relieve the faithful from ensuring that the Mass they attend is "legitimately celebrated." Consequently, the faithful can fulfill the obligation of canon 1248, §1 even at Masses illegitimately celebrated.

Regardless of how this issue is resolved, one thing is certain in the meantime: the remission of excommunication of the four bishops illicitly ordained by Archbishop Lefebvre in no way alters the juridic status of the SSPX or the ministry exercised by its clerics. The circumstances of the SSPX and the implications of canon 1248, §1 were clearly not foreseen at the time of the promulgation of the 1983 Code. The legislator may wish to issue a restrictive interpretation of canon 1248, §1, much like the authentic interpretations of canons 917 and 767, §1, determining under what circumstances the Mass obligation is properly fulfilled.[11] This would be especially beneficial to practitioners of the law, who grapple with the scope of canon 1248, §1, and those who frequent SSPX chapels. Ultimately, a satisfactory resolution will only be found through the re-establishment of full ecclesiastical communion with clerics of the SSPX, a clear objective of Pope

---

[11] See *Acta Apostolicae Sedis* 76 (1984) 746 and Acta Apostolicae Sedis 79 (1987) 1249 respectively.

Benedict XVI, and a task presently assigned to the Congregation for the Doctrine of the Faith.[12]

Chad J. Glendinning, J.C.L.

---

[12] See Pope Benedict XVI, Apostolic Letter, *motu proprio Ecclesiae Unitatem*, July 2, 2009 at http://www.vatican.va/holy_father/benedict_xvi/apost_letters/documents/hf_ben-xvi_apl_20090702_ecclesiae-unitatem_lt.html [accessed July 2009].

CANON 1285

DONATIONS AND STABLE PATRIMONY

One of our wealthier parishes recently received a large legacy when a parishioner died. The entire estate was given with the stipulation that it be used for purposes of charity and religion as these are identified by the pastor. With the consensus of both the parish pastoral council and the parish finance council, the pastor intends to donate $10,000 from the estate to an inner-city group which will use the funds to purchase property to establish a center for the homeless. Is the pastor, as the administrator of the parish, and without permission from the diocesan bishop, able to make this donation?

OPINION

This case concerns a charitable donation by an administrator (i.e., the pastor: see c. 532) of a public juridic person (i.e., a parish: see c. 515, §3). Such an act is governed by the norm of canon 1285, which states: "Within the limits of ordinary administration only, administrators are permitted to make donations for purposes of piety or Christian charity from movable goods which do not belong to the stable patrimony." Although there seems to be no doubt that this charitable donation would respect the intention of the donor (see c. 1300), the answer to the question depends on two factors: (1) whether or not making such a charitable donation would constitute an act of extraordinary administration; and (2) whether or not the legacy has been designated as *stable patrimony*. Both these issues merit further canonical consideration.

1 – Extraordinary Parish Administration

The *Code of Canon Law* distinguishes acts of *ordinary* administration and acts of *extraordinary* administration.[1]

---

[1] For the juridic person of a diocese (see c. 373), the Code also distinguishes acts of ordinary administration "which are more important in light of the economic condition of the diocese" (c. 1277). These are determined by the diocesan bishop himself; the law does not require that he consult anyone to make this determination, though he may prudently select to do so freely. To perform such acts, he needs the advice (but not the consent) of both the diocesan finance council and the college of consultors.

Acts of *ordinary* administration are those which are done routinely in order to maintain ecclesiastical goods. Canon 1284, §2 offers examples of activities involved in acts of ordinary administration. Commentators commonly identify as acts of ordinary administration such tasks as: "the collection of debts, rents, interests or dividends; contracts and payments necessary for the ordinary maintenance of the church and its personnel; the opening of checking accounts to facilitate these payments; and the acceptance of ordinary donations."[2] Put quite simply, acts of ordinary administration involve "the normal transaction of business by the canonical stewards of a public juridic person, i.e., things done routinely or regularly."[3]

Acts of *extraordinary* administration are all others–that is, acts which do not routinely occur, acts "which exceed the limits and manner of ordinary administration" (c. 1281, §1). Jordan Hite says that acts of extraordinary administration "are those which because of the nature or importance of the action or its financial value require the permission of a higher authority. Examples would include ... acceptance or refusal of major bequests or gifts, purchase of land, construction of new buildings or extensive repair of old buildings, initial investment of capital, other expenditures of an amount over a certain limit."[4]

Acts of extraordinary administration of public juridic persons (such as parishes) must be clearly defined. Typically, the statutes of a juridic person define acts of extraordinary administration. If the statutes are silent, however, the diocesan bishop is competent to determine such acts for the juridic persons subject to him, after he has received the advice of the diocesan finance council (see c. 1281, §2).[5] In order to perform *validly* an act of extraordinary administration (whether such an act is determined by statutes or the diocesan bishop), without prejudice to the statutes, the administrator of the public juridic person must first have obtained the written faculty (*facultas scripto*

---

[2] John A. Abbo and Jerome D. Hannan, *The Sacred Canons: A Concise Presentation of the Current Disciplinary Norms of the Church*, 2 vols. (Saint Louis: B. Herder Book Co., 1952), 2:731. See also T. Lincoln Bouscaren, Adam Ellis, and Francis N. Korth, *Canon Law: A Text and Commentary*, 4th rev. ed. (Milwaukee: Bruce Publishing Co., 1963), 829-830; Georges Vromant, *De bonis Ecclesiae temporalibus*, 3rd rev. ed. (Brussels: Éditions De Schuet, 1953), 161.

[3] J. Adam Maida and Nicholas P. Cafardi, *Church Property, Church Finances, and Church-Related Corporations* (Saint Louis: The Catholic Health Association of the United States, 1984), 301-302. The authors give the following examples: "maintaining property and checking accounts, receiving rent or interest income, accepting nominal gifts, paying bills, and making routine sales and purchases," 302.

[4] Jordan Hite, "Church Law on Property and Contracts," *The Jurist* 44 (1984) 121.

[5] For the juridic person of the diocese, the conference of bishops determines acts of extraordinary administration (c. 1277).

data) of the ordinary (c. 1281, §1).[6] For the pastor of a parish to perform such an act concerning parochial goods, he needs the written faculty of the local ordinary (see c. 134, §2).

2 – Stable Patrimony

Two canons in *Book V: The Temporal Goods of the Church* of the 1983 Code refer to "stable patrimony," a term that had not appeared in the 1917 Code. Canon 1285, mentioned above, says that charitable donations cannot be made from stable patrimony. Canon 1291 says that permission from competent ecclesiastical authority is required for the valid alienation of ecclesiastical goods that constitute, by legitimate designation, the stable patrimony of a public juridic person and whose value exceeds the sum defined by law. In addition, canon 1295 says that canons 1291-1294 (governing alienation) must be observed also in transactions (other than alienations) that can worsen the "patrimonial condition" of a public juridic person. Finally, canon 1283 requires administrators of public juridic persons to make and update an accurate and clear inventory that identifies its patrimony. Interestingly, canon 1026 of the *Code of Canons of the Eastern Churches* (which corresponds to *CIC* c. 1283) states specifically that the regularly updated inventory is to note changes in "stable" patrimony.

The term "stable patrimony" did not appear in the 1917 Code. The *coetus* revising the earlier law chose this term to replace the phrase "immovable ecclesiastical goods and movable ecclesiastical goods which can be saved by preserving them" (*res ecclesiasticas immobiles et mobiles, quae servando servari possunt*), a phrase found in canon 1530, §1 of the 1917 Code.[7] This term was selected in the midst of discussion on the need for permission from a higher authority to alienate ecclesiastical goods, immovable and movable. The *coetus* explained that the purpose of the law is not to hinder alienation of goods that can be saved by preserving them, but instead to exercise caution lest the stable patrimony of the Church be imprudently dissipated by

---

[6] For the diocesan bishop to perform acts of extraordinary diocesan administration, he must have the consent (not merely the advice) of the diocesan finance council and the college of consultors (c 1277).

[7] See Velasio DePaolis, *De bonis Ecclesiae temporalibus: Adnotationes in Codicem, Liber V* (Rome: Gregorian University, 1986), 101; Yuji Sugawara, "Amministrazione e alienazione dei beni temporali nel Codice (can. 638)," *Periodica*, 97 (2008) 269.

administrators. The *coetus* identified cash as among movable goods that can be designated as stable patrimony.[8]

The introduction of the term "stable patrimony" into current legislation has many practical implications. For example, the very wording of canons 1283, 1285, 1291, and 1295 implies that every juridic person must at least have the capacity to possess stable patrimony (see also c. 114, §3, which says competent ecclesiastical authority may confer juridic personality only on aggregates "which pursue a truly useful purpose and, all things considered, possess the means which are foreseen to be sufficient to achieve their designated purpose," that is, the means necessary for at least eventual financial self-sufficiency[9]). Stable patrimony comes into existence by lawful designation; it can never come into existence "accidentally." Absent proof that an ecclesiastical good is stable patrimony, one will presume that it is non-stable patrimony. Admittedly, such a presumption yields to contrary proof (see c. 1584). Canonists conclude that designating stable patrimony is an act of *extraordinary* administration.[10] This means that the pastor, inasmuch as he is the administrator of the parish, is the agent competent to designate the stable patrimony of the parish; to do so validly, however, he must first have received the written faculty of the local ordinary (without prejudice to the parochial statutes).

Certain goods by their very nature should be designated as stable patrimony: for example, real estate belonging to and used by public juridic persons (land, churches, schools, hospitals), designated or restricted funds (e.g., retirement funds, endowments, building funds), etc.[11] Particular (diocesan) law would wisely identify these goods, so administrators will legitimately designate them accordingly. It would be an abuse of ecclesiastical office (see c. 1389) for an administrator to refuse to designate a good as stable

---

[8] *Communicationes* 37 (2005) 120-121.

[9] Jean-Pierre Schouppe, *Droit canonique des biens* (Montréal: Wilson and Lafleur, 2008), 156.

[10] Velasio DePaolis states clearly: "We can ... say that designating some goods as stable patrimony is an act of extraordinary administration." See "Negozio giuidico, 'quo conditio patrimonialis personae iuridicae peior fieri possit' (see c. 1295)," *Periodica* 83 (1994) 523. See also V. DePaolis, *De bonis Ecclesiae temporalibus*, 101; V. DePaolis, *I Beni Temporali della Chiesa* (Bologna: Dehoniane, 1995), 187; Schouppe, 156.

[11] Some may suggest that goods such as these are implicitly stable patrimony. Nonetheless, inasmuch as canon 1291 says that stable patrimony is constituted by legitimate designation, it appears that stable patrimony must be explicitly identified. Such explicit designation avoids confusion when subsequently investigating whether or not an ecclesiastical good is stable patrimony.

patrimony if it should be so designated (e.g., in order to circumvent the need to obtain consent to alienate it).

Goods designated as stable patrimony are not forever "frozen": they can be alienated, but in some cases such alienation requires consent from higher authorities (see c. 1292; see also c. 1295). Further, stable patrimony can be converted into non-stable patrimony; inasmuch as such conversion involves alienation, however, the norms of canons 1291-1294 must be observed. Also, immovable goods belonging to stable patrimony can be transformed from movable goods belonging to stable patrimony, and vice versa; nonetheless, when such transformation involves alienation of real estate, the norms of canons 1291-1294 are to be observed.[12]

Donors (see c. 1299, §1) may request that their gifts become part of stable patrimony. If such is the case, these donations carry a modal obligation (if not a condition), and the administrator must receive the permission of the ordinary before accepting them (c. 1267, §2).

Finally, ecclesiastical goods designated as stable patrimony are not subject to diocesan taxation. Canon 1263 allows the diocesan bishop to impose an ordinary or extraordinary diocesan tax. The ordinary tax (*tributum*) can be imposed "for the needs of the diocese" and the extraordinary tax (*exactio*) can be imposed "in case of grave necessity." Either tax must be moderate and proportionate to the income of the person upon whom it is levied, and can be imposed only after the diocesan bishop receives the advice of the diocesan

---

[12] Francis G. Morrisey, O.M.I. reflects: "The exchange of securities for securities is generally not governed by the prescriptions on alienation. The norms on administration would apply. If, however, title to real estate is transferred, this is alienation in the strict sense, unless the transfer was for another piece of real estate of the same value (in which case the situation of the ecclesiastical goods is not jeopardized). There are, however, differences of opinion regarding the following case of transfer: some canonists accept that in cases where the sound administration of the goods of the entire juridical person requires that it be unburdened of certain pieces of property, such as land which may no longer be used for Church purposes, vacant land being heavily taxed, land creating ill will toward the Church and its credibility on social concerns, etc., the norms on alienation would not be applicable. Personally, I feel that such situations would give rise to a legitimate cause for alienation (see c. 1293), but that the transfer would be subject to the prescriptions governing alienation." See "The Alienation of Temporal Goods in Contemporary Practice," *Studia canonica* 29 (1995) 308.
John J. Myers reaches the same conclusion: "If property, including stocks and bonds, is exchanged for property of approximately equal value, no alienation occurs. Transfer of title in exchange for something in a different category, however, is alienation. Some hold that if property were to be sold with the proceeds to be designated as part of the stable patrimony, alienation would not occur. The Code, however, seems to consider any sale of real estate as alienation and subject to the regulations" concerning alienation. See "The Temporal Goods of the Church," in *The Code of Canon Law: Text and Commentary*, eds. James A. Coriden, Thomas J. Green, and Donald E. Heintschel (New York: Paulist Press, 1985), 883.

finance council and the presbyteral council. Inasmuch as the tax is to be imposed upon income only, goods designated as stable patrimony cannot be taxed, though income accruing from them can be.

In summary, the distinction between stable patrimony and non-stable patrimony is the *fundamental* distinction between all ecclesiastical goods in the current universal law.[13] This distinction determines:

- what consent from higher authorities is needed to alienate certain goods
- what is to be protected in potentially threatening transactions other than alienation
- what is subject to diocesan taxation and
- what is able to be donated for pious or charitable purposes.

Regularly updated inventories must clearly identify goods belonging to stable patrimony, distinguishing them from non-stable patrimony.

If the pastor wishes to donate $10,000 from the estate for a charitable purpose, he will need to learn if a donation of such size constitutes an act of extraordinary administration as determined by the diocesan bishop. If such is the case, the pastor will need the written faculty of the local ordinary before proceeding. Further, if the money has been legitimately assigned to the stable patrimony of the parish, he cannot donate it for a charitable purpose.

Rev. Msgr. John A. Renken, J.C.D.

---

[13] Canonists have commonly distinguished ecclesiastical goods in a variety of ways: e.g., movable/immovable, corporeal/incorporeal, sacred/profane, precious/non-precious, etc. In light of the 1983 Code, canonists would also distinguish all ecclesiastical goods as stable/non-stable patrimony.

CANONS 1395 AND 19

APPLICATION OF THE *ESSENTIAL NORMS* IN CASES OF DOUBT

The 2006 "Essential Norms for Diocesan/Eparchial Policies Dealing with Allegations of Sexual Abuse of Minors by Priests of Deacons" direct that, in cases of doubt as to whether specific behaviors constitute an offense under canon 1395, "the writings of recognized moral theologians should be consulted." Can you make some specific suggestions as to how such consultation could be conducted?

OPINION

The moral theology aspects of clergy sexual misconduct cases are important not only for applying the *Essential Norms* correctly,[1] but for understanding canon 1395 of the 1983 *Code of Canon Law*, its Pio-Benedictine predecessors, and several other ecclesiastical documents.[2] William H. Woestman, O.M.I. recently underscored the need for canonists to come to grips with the moral tradition on sexual misconduct,[3] but he did not make specific suggestions as to authors. I will offer some below. A few preliminary points should be made.

---

[1] "If there is any doubt whether a specific act qualifies as an external, objectively grave violation [of the sixth commandment of the Decalogue], the writings of recognized moral theologians should be consulted, and the opinions of recognized experts should be appropriately obtained." United States Conference of Catholic Bishops, "Essential Norms for Diocesan/Eparchial Policies Dealing with Allegations of Sexual Abuse of Minors by Priests or Deacons" (Washington, DC: United States Conference of Catholic Bishops, 2006), footnote 2, available at http://www.usccb.org/ocyp/ 2005EssentialNorms.pdf [accessed June 2009].

[2] "Sub luce igitur principiorum iuris atque interpretationis canonicae, unaque cum normis e morali theologia haustis, vigentes hodie ecclesiasticae leges in materia sollicitationis examine subiicientur, ut certa ab incertis, solide probabiles a fundamento destitutis opinionibus sedulo distinguentes, tum littera tum sensus legum earumque ad praxim applicatio, clarius cognoscatur." Juan Ortega Uhink, *De Delicto Sollicitationis*, *Canon Law Studies No. 289* (Washington, DC: Catholic University of America Press, 1954), 129. There is no reason to limit Uhink's observation to Pio-Benedictine solicitation cases. For examples of other ecclesiastical documents for which moral theology categories are relevant, see, e.g., Pope John Paul II, *motu proprio Sacramentorum sanctitatis tutela*, April 30, 2001, *Acta Apostolicae Sedis* 93 (2001) 737-739; National Conference of Catholic Bishops, *Canonical Delicts Involving Sexual Misconduct and Dismissal From the Clerical State* (Washington, DC: United States Catholic Conference, 1995), 6; or Supremae Sacrae Congregationis Sancti Offici, *Instructio de Modo Procedendi in Causis Sollicitationis, Crimen Sollicitationis*, March 16, 1962 (Vatican City: Typis Polyglottis Vaticanis, 1962), nos. 71 and 73.

[3] William H. Woestman, O.M.I., "An Offense Against the Sixth Commandment of the Decalogue," in *Roman Replies and CLSA Advisory Opinions 2006*, eds. F. Stephen Pedone and Paul D. Counce (Alexandria, VA: Canon Law Society of America, 2006), 86-88.

First, one must realize that the modern canons on penal law were in place by quite early in the post-Conciliar reform process, having been drafted by men steeped in the dominant pre-conciliar method of doing moral theology known as the "manualist tradition."[4] One must understand how moral writers and commentators approached these issues yesterday in order to advise better canonical decision-makers today. For example, to understand the phrase in canon 1395, §1 threatening punishment of those persisting "with scandal in another external sin against the sixth commandment of the Decalogue," one must be aware, as were the canonists who drafted those canons, of the moral tradition that: (1) understood *scandal* in a way quite differently from how it is used in common parlance; (2) took for granted several distinctions between *external* sins and *internal* sins; (3) saw the sixth commandment as upholding the virtue of *chastity* while the ninth commandant worked in service to *modesty*; (4) knew what it meant (and did not mean) to say that "sins against chastity admit no parvity of matter," and so on.

Second, the cautionary language in canon 19 about not using "the common and constant opinion of learned persons" in penal matters does not mean that one cannot consult older authors for guidance in understanding the law on penal cases (indeed, one often must do so in accord with c. 17); rather, canon 19 forbids parleying *moral* offenses into canonical *crimes* by, say, logical extension or analogy with other delicts. Obviously, that is not what the *Essential Norms* are calling for here: Canon 1395 itself accords canonical consequences to certain kinds of offenses, while the *Essential Norms* simply direct consultation with moral theology authors in order to identify more precisely what the offenses scored by law are.

Third, although the *Essential Norms* use the phrase "recognized authors," it would probably have been better to describe such consultation in terms of "approved authors" (*auctores probati*) rather than "recognized authors." There are several reasons for this, not the least of which is that it approaches this subject matter on its own terms rather than imposing on it more delicate, and sometimes more ambiguous, terminology from a later period. The simple fact is that the pool of "recognized authors" is necessarily wider than is the pool of

---

[4] On the "manualist tradition," see generally, Charles E. Curran, *Moral Theology at the End of the Century* (Milwaukee, WI: Marquette University Press, 1999), especially 1-34. Not all moral theologians writing before the Second Vatican Council were manualists, of course. See, e.g., Bernhard Häring, *The Law of Christ* (Westminster, MD: Newman Press, 1961), in 3 volumes. Most penal canons of the 1983 Code were in place no later than 1973. See Edward N. Peters, *Incrementa in Progressu 1983 Codicis Iuris Canonici: A Legislative History of the Code of Canon Law* (Montréal: Wilson & Lafleur, 2005), 1135-1197, especially 1195.

"approved authors," but it is the group known as "approved authors" that the architects of the 1983 Code would have had in mind when drafting norms on sexual misconduct cases. This means, in turn, that one must study materials generated almost entirely before the Second Vatican Council and that a large portion of those materials will be available only in Latin. Given that a fair number of important moralists writing before Vatican II were well trained in canon law, canonists consulting them today enjoy some affinity with them. It is to these authors that I will now provide some introduction.

As a practical matter, most American canonists will turn first to authors writing in English for an orientation to the moral-canonical issues they are researching. In my opinion, the single best place to begin any English-language canonically-oriented research into moral issues is Henry Davis, S.J. (English Jesuit, 1866-1952),[5] whose justly renowned *Moral and Pastoral Theology* was published, in four volumes, by Sheed and Ward beginning in 1934.[6] Davis knows the manualist tradition intimately. He ably weaves canonical considerations into his moral analysis, tries to keep a good eye on pastoral questions (especially in matters likely to arise in confession), and does not overload his text with footnotes. Davis is, moreover, an excellent starting point from which one can, if desired, go back to older English-language sources–such as Thomas Slater, S.J. (English Jesuit, 1855-1928),[7] *Questions of Moral Theology* (1908/1915), or to co-authors John A. McHugh, O.P. (American Dominican, 1880-1950)[8] and Charles J. Callan, O.P. (American

---

[5] See T. Corbishley, "Davis, Henry," *New Catholic Encyclopedia*, 2nd ed. (Detroit, MI: Thomsan/Gale Group, 2003), IV: 544-545. Although 99% of Davis' material is in English, he wrote about certain sexual issues in Latin, doubtless out of a sense of propriety.

[6] Most manualist theologians published multiple editions of their works with only slight changes from edition to edition. It is well to keep track of, then, besides what edition one is consulting and what page number, the topic or paragraph number of a given subject, if one is given, because topic numbers tended to remain more constant. Also, be aware that many works were known not only by the last name of the original author (e.g., "Génicot" or "Noldin"), but by the author and the later editors or redactors of their works (e.g., "Génicot-Salsman" or "Noldin-Schmidt"). This can be confusing because some works, such as Ford and Kelly, were jointly penned by two different authors. Exposure to the works will make such distinctions clear.

[7] See J. Bischoff, "Slater, Thomas," *New Catholic Encyclopedia* (New York: McGraw-Hill, 1967), XIII: 280, and R. Brouillard, *Dictionnaire de Théologie Catholique* (Paris: Letouzey et Ané, 1941), XIV/2: 2245-2246. Slater has a number of other monographs on specific moral theology topics besides his famous, and more general, English text.

[8] See J. Phelps, "McHugh, John Ambrose," *New Catholic Encyclopedia* (New York: McGraw Hill, 1967), IX: 35, and John Delaney, *Dictionary of American Catholic Biography* (Garden City, NY: Doubleday, 1984), 371.

Dominican, 1877-1962),[9] *Moral Theology*, in two volumes (1929). Or, one can move forward to English-language authors writing just before Vatican II, especially to co-authors John C. Ford, S.J. (American Jesuit, 1902-1989)[10] and Gerald Kelly, S.J. (American Jesuit, 1902-1964),[11] *Contemporary Moral Theology*, in two volumes (1958-1963), or Francis J. Connell, C.Ss.R. (American Redemptorist, 1888-1967),[12] *Outlines of Moral Theology*, 2nd edition (1958). Finally, from Davis one can move across, as is usually eventually necessary, to the major Latin-language moral theology authors.

The saintly Roman Jesuit Felix M. Cappello, S.J. (1879-1962)[13] published his famous *Tractatus Canonico-Moralis de Sacramentis* during the 1920s and 1930s, in five volumes, with the seventh and final edition appearing in 1962 on the eve of the Council. Cappello is by far my preferred consultation source among the Latin-language canonico-moralists. Essentially a canonist who also did fine work in morals, Cappello is the epitome of scholars who reverence tradition without losing track of the values that tradition is meant to serve. One who disagrees with Cappello's analysis on this or that point bears a heavy burden of proof. Then, second only to Cappello, I would consult his co-religionist, the Belgian Jesuit Arthur Vermeersch, S.J. (1858-1936),[14] essentially a moralist who also did fine work as a canonist, who is best known for his *Theologiae Moralis Principia, Responsa, Consilia* (1922/1924), in four volumes.

---

[9] See J. Coffey, "Callahan, Charles Jerome," *New Catholic Encyclopedia*, 2nd ed. (Detroit, MI: Thomson/Gale Group, 2003), II: 876, and John Delaney, *Dictionary of American Catholic Biography* (Garden City, NY: Doubleday, 1984), 81.

[10] See Eric Genilo, *John Cutherbert Ford: Moral Theologian at the End of the Manualist Era* (Washington, DC: Georgetown University Press, 2007), passim. Although Ford was not a paradigmatic manualist, and although I am not convinced that Genilo fully understood the context in which Ford worked, Genilo's study is a useful introduction to Ford and to the wider manualist method.

[11] See C. McAuliffe, "Kelly, Gerard Andrew," *New Catholic Encyclopedia*, 2nd ed. (Detroit, MI: Thomson/Gale Group, 2003), VIII: 139, and John Delaney, *Dictionary of American Catholic Biography* (Garden City, NY: Doubleday, 1984), 290. See also Edwin Lisson, *The Historical Context and Sources of Moral Theology in the Writings of Gerald A. Kelly, S.J.* (Rome: Gregorian, 1975).

[12] See L. Riley, "Connell, Francis J.," *New Catholic Encyclopedia*, 2nd ed. (Detroit, MI: Thomson/Gale Group, 2003), IV: 126, and John Delaney, *Dictionary of American Catholic Biography* (Garden City, NY: Doubleday, 1984), 108.

[13] See Petrus Huizing, "In memoriam Felicis Mariae Cappello S.J.," *Periodica* 51 (1962) 410-412. For a bibliography of Cappello's work through 1958, see anon., "Scripta R. P. F. M. Cappello S.I.," *Periodica* 48 (1959) vii-xxiv.

[14] See J. Upton, "Vermeersch, Arthur," *New Catholic Encyclopedia*, 2nd ed. (Detroit, MI: Thomson/Gale Group, 2003), XIV: 452-453; Joseph Creusen, *Le Père Arthur Vermeersch, S.J.: L'homme et l'oeuvre* (1947); and anon., "[Arcturus Vermeersch S.J.]," *Jus Pontificium* 17 (1937) 106-110.

Besides these two classic Latin language authors, *many* other experts could be listed. In alphabetical order, some that I have found useful would include:

- Joseph Aertnys, S.J. (Dutch Jesuit, 1828-1915),[15] *Theologia Moralis Secundum Doctrinam S. Alphonsi, de Ligorio, Doctoris Ecclesi* (1886/1887), in two volumes
- Giuseppe D'Annibale (Italian cardinal, 1815-1892),[16] *Summula Theologiae Moralis*, (1881-1883), in three volumes
- Eduard Génicot, S.J. (Belgian Jesuit, 1856-1900),[17] *Theologiae Moralis Institutionis* (1896) and his *Casus Conscientiae* (1901)
- Augustino Lehmkuhl, S.J. (German Jesuit, 1834-1918),[18] with two major works, *Theologia Moralis* (1883), in two volumes, and *Casus Conscientiae ad Usum Confessariorum Compositi et Soluti* (1902-1904), also in two volumes
- Benoît Henri Merkelbach, O.P. (Belgian Dominican, 1871-1942),[19] *Summa Theologiae Moralis* (1931-1940), in three volumes, and *Quaestiones de Castitate et Luxuria Quas in Utilitatem Cleri* (1936)
- Jerome Noldin, S.J. (Austrian Jesuit, 1838-1922),[20] *Summa Theologiae Moralis* (1902) in three volumes
- Dominicus Prümmer, O.P. (Austrian Dominican, 1866-1931),[21] *Manuale Theologiae Moralis* (1914), in three volumes, and *Vademecum Theologiae Moralis* (1921), the fifth/sixth edition of which was translated into English by Gerald Shelton and published under the title *Handbook of Moral Theology* (1956)

---

[15] See A. Sampers, "Aertnys, Jozef," *New Catholic Encyclopedia*, 2nd ed. (Detroit, MI: Thomson/Gale Group, 2003), I: 140.
[16] See P. Mulhern, "Annibale, Giuseppe," *New Catholic Encyclopedia* (New York: McGraw Hill, 1967), I: 561, and A. Beugnet, *Dictionnaire de Théologie Catholique* (Paris: Letouzey et Ané, 1923), I/1:1322.
[17] See J. Campana, "Génicot, Éduoard," *New Catholic Encyclopedia*, 2nd ed. (Detroit, MI: Thomson/Gale Group, 2003), VI:135, and P. Bernard, *Dictionnaire de Théologie Catholique* (Paris: Letouzey et Ané, 1924), VI/1:1223-1224.
[18] R. Bush, "Lehmkuhl, August," *New Catholic Encyclopedia* (New York: McGraw Hill, 1967), VIII: 619.
[19] See C. Lozier, "Merkelbach, Benoît Henri," *New Catholic Encyclopedia* (New York: McGraw Hill, 1967), IX: 686.
[20] See J. Upton, "Noldin, Hieronymus," *New Catholic Encyclopedia*, 2nd ed. (Detroit, MI: Thomson/Gale Group, 2003), X: 409-410.
[21] See generally C. Lozier, "Prümmer, Dominikus," *New Catholic Encyclopedia*, 2nd ed. (Detroit, MI: Thomson/Gale Group, 2003), XI: 793-794, and anon., "In memoriam [D. Prümmer]," *Jus Pontificium* 11 (1931) 119-121.

- Aloysius Sabetti, S.J. (Italian Jesuit, 1839-1898),[22] *Compendium Theologiae Moralis* (1884), in two volumes.

Finally, although not writing his moral works primarily in Latin, Heribert Jone, O.F.M. Cap. (German Capuchin, 1885-1967),[23] who published his *Katholische Moraltheologie* in 1930, should certainly be mentioned, as his respected text was translated into English by Urban Adelman, O.F.M., Cap. and appeared widely during the 1940s and 1950s under the simple title *Moral Theology*.

Brief mention can also be made of two moral theology dictionaries that appeared late in the manualist era, namely, Pietro Palazzini's *Dictionarium Morale et Canonicum* (1962-1968), in four volumes, and Francesco Roberti's *Dictionary of Moral Theology* (1962, being an English translation of the 1954 Italian original). Occasionally, I think, useful moral information can be found in Palazzini's dictionary (though I much prefer the canonical entries therein), but one could, in my opinion, safely skip Roberti's moral dictionary without fear of missing anything unique.

While an orientation to theologians and works is helpful, only extended consultation with the materials themselves will enable one to arrive at an understanding of how the manualist method impacted canonical thinking. I could say that, broadly speaking, manualist moral theologians followed one of two philosophical schools (those of Sts. Alphonsus Ligouri and Thomas Aquinas) but by no means are manualists simply defenders of their own school and opponents of the other. Even less are they parrots of one another within a single discipline. The debates among manualists were lively, if more subtle than many of us are accustomed to today, and the insights they developed remain useful not simply to canonists, but to all those striving to use the mind to assess and direct human conduct.

Edward N. Peters, J.D., J.C.D.

---

[22] See J. Hennesey, "Sabetti, Aloysius," *New Catholic Encyclopedia*, 2nd ed. (Detroit, MI: Thomson/Gale Group, 2003), XII: 462, and R. Brouillard, *Dictionnaire de Théologie Catholique* (Paris: Letouzey et Ané, 1939), XIV/1:438.

[23] See Wilhelm Lederer, *Pater Dr. Heribert Jone: Ein Leben für Gott und die Wissenschaft* (Schelklinger Hefte: Stadtarchiv, 1988), 13.

Canons 1444 and 1682, §2

APPEAL OF MARRIAGE NULLITY CASES BEFORE THE TRIBUNAL OF THE ROMAN ROTA

Once a case has been appealed in second instance to the Tribunal of the Roman Rota, must the parties take any initiatives in prosecuting the appeal, or does the appeal proceed in second instance by the law itself?

OPINION

There are three places to look to find the answer to this question: The 1983 *Code of Canon Law*; the April 18, 1994 "Norms of the Tribunal of the Roman Rota"; and the January 25, 2005 Instruction of the Pontifical Council for Legislative Texts, *Dignitas Connubii*. In the end, the "Norms of the Tribunal of the Roman Rota" will prove most helpful in answering the question.[1]

Canon 1682, §2 states that after an affirmative decision in first instance, the appellate tribunal has two options: to confirm by decree the affirmative sentence; or to admit the case to an ordinary examination in second instance. This was a change from the 1917 *Code of Canon Law*, which required the defender of the bond to appeal every affirmative decision. In the development of jurisprudence since the 1917 Code, however, it became clearer that the defender of the bond, and indeed all the officials of the tribunal, were to offer their opinions *pro rei veritate*. This was referred to particularly in the famous 1944 papal allocution to the Sacred Roman Rota by Pope Pius XII concerning the duties of the defender of the bond.[2] Therefore, in the development of this particular canon, the discussion moved from the appeal being prosecuted by the defender of the bond, to the appeal being prosecuted *ex officio* by the law itself. The defender of the bond, and the parties themselves, may also submit "observations" (*animadversiones*), but the appeal would go forward even without such observations.

The Instruction *Dignitas Connubii* adds nothing new to the prescriptions of canon 1682, §2. Article 264 states that an affirmative sentence must be sent to

---

[1] An unofficial English translation of the 1994 "Norms of the Tribunal of the Roman Rota" may be found in the *Exegetical Commentary on the Code of Canon Law*, eds. Ángel Marzoa, Jorge Miras, and Rafael Rodríguez-Ocaña (Montréal: Wilson & Lafleur, 2004), V: 257-288.

[2] Pope Pius XII, Allocution to the Sacred Roman Rota, October 2, 1944, *Acta Apostolicae Sedis* 36 (1944) 281-290; English translation in *Canon Law Digest* 3:612-622.

the appellate tribunal *ex officio*, thus continuing the appeal by the law itself. Article 265 gives the parties the option of proposing observations to the appellate court, with the caution that the court of appeal must respond to any observations that have been submitted. Article 266 clarifies that a negative decision cannot be confirmed by a decree of the second instance court, but must be heard by an ordinary examination in second instance, if an appeal has been lodged by the party who feels aggrieved by the negative decision. Canon 1682, §2 had indicated what options were available if an affirmative decision had been rendered in first instance, but had not treated specifically what would happen if the decision in first instance had been negative. For those decisions which did not find for the nullity of the marriage, a party who disagreed with the decision would have to refer to canons 1628 and following for further instruction. Article 266, along with article 279, gathers together the prescriptions of canons 1628 and 1682 to assist tribunal personnel in following the proper procedures.

If the affirmative sentence of the first instance court is confirmed by the appellate court by decree, the special procedures for marriage nullity cases in the 1983 Code are silent on what recourse a party might have. Under the title of *Res iudicata,* canon 1644 provides for the appeal of two conforming sentences in cases involving the status of persons, but it is not clear that this would apply equally to a sentence that was confirmed by decree. However, article 290 of *Dignitas Connubii* allows for the petition for an examination of the same cause after two conforming decisions, regardless of whether they are sentences or decrees, stating that either "can be challenged at any time before a tribunal of third or higher instance, as long as new and grave proofs or arguments have been brought forward within the peremptory time limit of thirty days from the time the challenge was proposed" (§1).[3]

Likewise, the law is silent on any recourse against a decree admitting the case to an ordinary hearing in second instance. *Dignitas Connubii* provides no further instruction on this matter, although the commentator Carmelo de Diego-Lora states, "This decree cannot be appealed because it does not have the force of a definitive sentence and will therefore be among those excluded from appeal by c. 1629, 4°."[4]

---

[3] Klaus Lüdicke and Ronny E. Jenkins, *Dignitas Connubii: Norms and Commentary* (Washington, DC: Canon Law Society of America, 2006), 465.

[4] Carmelo de Diego-Lara, Commentary on Canon 1682, in *Exegetical Commentary on the Code of Canon Law*, eds. Ángel Marzoa, Jorge Miras, and Rafael Rodríguez-Ocaña (Montréal: Wilson & Lafleur, 2004), IV/2:1852.

With regard to hearing a case by means of the ordinary process in second instance, both the 1983 Code and *Dignitas Connubii* are vague. Canon 1640 states that the appellate procedure is the same as the first instance procedure "with appropriate adjustments" (*congrua congruis referendo)*; article 267, §1 of the Instruction uses the same terminology. Neither text indicates what those appropriate adjustments might be.

The "Norms of the Tribunal of the Roman Rota" contain a further explanation of how this will take place, at least in cases before the Roman Rota. Title III of these Norms details how the Roman Rota proceeds with cases, including at the appellate level.

It would go beyond the scope of this advisory opinion to go through the details of this Title. What is of greatest and most immediate interest to canonists who may be assisting those whose cases were appealed to the Roman Rota in second instance can be found in article 58, §2. After stating that the *turnus* will either confirm the decision of the first instance court, or "propose definitely and individually motives which stand in the way of the nullity and therefore admit the case to ordinary examination at a new grade," the Norm states that "the *ponens*, with the will of the parties known about the prosecution of the case, will take care to move the case ahead...."[5]

It is the phrase, "with the will of the parties known about the prosecution of the case" (*cognita partium voluntate de iudicio prosequendo*) that is most important. For most second instance cases, the prosecution of the appeal proceeds automatically. This is not true of cases heard at the Tribunal of the Roman Rota. In these cases, the parties must make their intention known that they wish to prosecute the matter further. In the absence of any manifestation of will on the part of at least one of the parties, the action will be abated after one year, according to article 65 of the Norms.

The instruction about this matter is usually contained in the decree that states that the first instance sentence cannot be confirmed and that the case must be admitted to the ordinary process in second instance. It is not always reflected in the cover letter that accompanies the decree, so the judicial vicar must be clear in his instructions to the parties, informing them that if they wish the case to proceed, they must indicate this to the *ponens*. The judicial vicar, of course, can assist the parties in making their intentions known. But without a

---

[5] "Norms of the Tribunal of the Roman Rota," in *Exegetical Commentary on the Code of Canon Law*, V:274.

clear manifestation of the intention of at least one of the parties, the action will be abated and the case will be placed in the Rotal archives.

On a final note, article 19, §2 of *Dignitas Connubii* states that in cases of abatement, renunciation, or desertion before the Roman Rota, if the cause is to be resumed, it must be before that same Tribunal. This, of course, applies only to causes that would be introduced on the same grounds. If the petition were to be introduced on new grounds, it could be heard through the normal first instance tribunal.

Rev. Patrick R. Lagges, J.C.D.

Canons 1481 and 1620, 7°

Awareness of the Right to Appoint an Advocate as Essential to the Right of Defense

A person in a marriage case petitions a tribunal for a declaration of nullity but is never informed that he or she can seek the assistance of an advocate. Furthermore, the person is unaware that he or she has the right to request the assistance of an advocate. Later, the person asserts that he or she did not understand anything about the case and was unable to carry out a competent presentation of the case, which resulted in a finding of non constat. *It also appears, upon further review, that the case was not well instructed and that there are facts that suggest nullity of consent. Can the first instance decision be declared null under canon 1620, 7°, based on a denial of the right of defense?*

Opinion

Canon 1481 of the 1983 *Code of Canon Law* and article 101 of the January 25, 2005 Instruction *Dignitas Connubii* (*DC*) provide the applicable principles regarding the right to an advocate in marriage cases. Under canon 1481, §1, "A party can freely appoint an advocate…." The party also has the right to "petition and respond personally unless the judge has decided that the services of a procurator or advocate are necessary." Implicit in this text is the notion that the party has been informed of the right to an advocate and has made a knowing waiver of the right; and further, that the judge can overturn that waiver if he thinks it necessary.

This is made even more clear in article 101, §1 of *DC*, which provides that the assistance of an advocate is considered to be more than just a casual option; the following language emphasizes the point: "...[T]he tribunal is bound by the obligation to provide that each spouse is able to defend his [or her] rights with the help of a competent person, most especially when it concerns causes of a special difficulty."[1] Article 113, §3 provides that each tribunal is to have "stable advocates designated" to assist the parties; the implication is that the parties should be made aware that such a person is available. Most tellingly, as in canon 1481, article 101, §2 of *DC* provides that

---

[1] See Klaus Lüdicke and Ronny E. Jenkins, *Dignitas Connubii: Norms and Commentary* (Washington, DC: Canon Law Society of America, 2006), 180.

the *praeses* is to assign an advocate even where a party has not named one in those cases where this seems necessary.

Antoni Stankiewicz provides salient teaching on the right to defense in his commentary to canon 1620, in which he states: "The right to defense, according to established jurisprudence, must be guaranteed to the parties in connection with its intactness (c. 1598 § 1), as well as with the ability to exercise it in the course of the canonical proceedings."[2] In addition to the right to be made aware of the proceedings, a party "also [has] the right to active confrontation through the presentation of one's own defense and evidence."[3]

The question remains, if a person is not competent to carry out his or her own defense, and the same person does not know of the right to request assistance in a case involving complicated Church procedures, how can he or she possibly exercise the "right to active confrontation through the presentation of one's own defense and evidence," as Stankiewicz states?

This dilemma was addressed in *coram* Burke, of May 22, 1997.[4] Burke makes reference to American "due process" as having an effect on the drafting of the 1983 Code regarding the protection of rights, in the context of canon 1620, 7°. Indeed, it is worth noting for our purposes that the right to the assistance of counsel is enshrined in the Sixth Amendment (within the Bill of Rights) to the U.S. Constitution: "In all criminal prosecutions, the accused shall enjoy the right . . . to have the Assistance of Counsel for his defence."[5] The U.S. Supreme Court has stated repeatedly that the right to counsel is "fundamental and essential to a fair trial." In *Gideon v. Wainright* (1963), the Supreme Court noted that "the right to be heard would be, in many cases, of little avail if it did not comprehend the right to be heard by counsel. Even the intelligent and educated layman has small and sometimes no skill in the science of law. . . .He lacks both the skill and knowledge adequately to prepare his defense, even though he have a perfect one."[6] The Court goes on to hold that not only must the State provide criminal defendants with an attorney, but it must provide one free of charge.

---

[2] Antoni Stankiewicz, Commentary on Canon 1620, in *Exegetical Commentary on the Code of Canon Law*, eds. Ángel Marzoa, Jorge Miras, and Rafael Rodríguez-Ocaña (Montréal: Wilson & Lafleur, 2004), IV/2:1549.

[3] Ibid.

[4] See *coram* Burke, May 22, 1997, in *Studia Canonica* 32 (1998) 515-524.

[5] The text of the Sixth Amendment is available at http://caselaw.lp.findlaw.com/data/constitution/amendment06/ [accessed June 2009].

[6] Gideon v. Wainwright, 372 U.S. 335 (1963), available at http://caselaw.lp.findlaw.com/scripts/getcase.pl?court=US&vol=372&invol=335 [accessed June 2009].

In a similar fashion, Burke maintains that the tribunal has an obligation to inform a party of his or her right to defend a marriage case, and that an omission of this duty can result in irremediable nullity under canon 1620, 7°:

> The right to defence is a technical notion, with a technical content. An obvious duty is incumbent therefore on the tribunal to inform each party of his or her right to defence, and to explain in clear and practical terms what it involves. Since the parties almost always possess little or no knowledge of canon law, not to inform them adequately of their rights is already to partially deny them those rights. A party may choose to waive the right of defence; but can be said to do so freely and responsibly, only if he or she has actually been informed of the main implications and modes of exercising this right.[7]

I therefore conclude that a tribunal that has not notified a party of the possibility of obtaining an advocate, or assigned one to assist the party (especially where the case is difficult, including those cases where the proofs are tenuous, as in the present case), has abridged the right of defense under canon 1620, 7°. The mere fact that a person petitions the tribunal should not act as a waiver of the right to the assistance of an advocate on the presumption that he or she is well aware of the procedures, since the average lay person is normally quite uninformed. Furthermore, it is clear from canon 1620, 7° that since the right of defense is due to "one or the other party," it clearly encompasses both the petitioner and the respondent.

Lawrence G. Price, J.D., J.C.L.

---

[7] See *coram* Burke, May 22, 1997, in *Studia Canonica* 32 (1998) 515-524.

CANONS 1620, 1°; 1620, 7°; AND 1622, 1°

IRREMEDIABLE NULLITY OF A DECREE ISSUED BY A FIRST INSTANCE TRIBUNAL

A first instance collegiate tribunal rendered an affirmative decision on the ground of grave defect of discretion of judgment on the part of petitioner. This decision was ratified by decree by the second instance tribunal of appeal. The respondent had never received any citation or communication from either tribunal from the beginning because the petitioner had deliberately given the wrong address of the respondent. The respondent complains to the first instance tribunal of this deceptive behavior of the petitioner.

Because the respondent brought this injustice to the notice of the first instance tribunal, the defender of the bond of that tribunal lodged a plaint of irremediable nullity against the first instance sentence. The original ponens being legitimately impeded, the substitute ponens (not the college) declared the first instance sentence and the subsequent decree of confirmation irremediably null on the ground of violation of the respondent's right of defence (c. 1620, 7°). Considering the case still under discussion, the first instance tribunal carried out a supplementary instruction of the case and then pronounced a negative decision in first instance.

The petitioner lodged before the appeal court a plaint of nullity against the decree which had declared the first two decisions irremediably null claiming that the respondent was aware of the process. The appeal court responded negatively to this plaint of nullity affirming that the respondent was unaware of the trial from the beginning.

The petitioner's advocate presented a plaint of nullity against the negative sentence given by the first instance tribunal on the ground of absolute incompetence of the judges. The appeal tribunal dismissed this plaint with a negative decision. The petitioner's advocate then lodged another plaint of remediable nullity against the decree declaring the original two sentences irremediably null on the ground that the said decision was not rendered by the college of judges but by the sole substitute judge and that the same decision was not pronounced by the original ponens. The appeal court again ruled negatively on the complaint of nullity.

The questions now asked are: Was everything in this case done in accord with the norm of law? Was there anything radically wrong in what the first and second instance tribunals did in this case after the respondent brought to the attention of the court the deliberate manipulation of the process by the petitioner?

OPINION

Because this is a real and complex case, it is important that we examine at least some of the fundamental juridic and procedural principles involved in it. Although this brief study will probably not do justice to the complex issues involved in the case, nevertheless a close look at some of the difficult questions may allow us to rethink some of the actions of our local tribunals.

1 – Consequences of *res iudicata*

Because a marriage nullity cause concerns the status of persons and, therefore, never becomes *res iudicata* (c. 1643; *Dignitas Connubii* [*DC*], art. 289, §1), nevertheless certain definitive juridic consequences result when two conforming decisions are rendered in the same cause, between the same parties, and on the same ground(s) of nullity. Thus, if the two conforming decisions are affirmative, the parties are free to marry as soon as they receive legitimate communication to that effect, unless there is a *vetitum* imposed by the tribunal, or a prohibition placed by the ordinary of the place on the person[s] (and this would affect only the liceity and not the validity of subsequent marriage[s]) (see c. 1684, §1; *DC*, art. 301). There is no *direct* challenge [appeal] against the double conforming decision (see c. 1642, §1; *DC,* art. 290, §1). In cases concerning the status of persons, the sentence can be challenged any time before a tribunal of third or higher instance in order to obtain a new proposition or hearing of the case (*nova causae propositio*) only if *new* and *grave* proofs and arguments are presented within the peremptory time limit of thirty days from the time the challenge was proposed (see c. 1644, §1; *DC*, art. 290, §1). But this recourse for a new hearing of the case does not suspend the execution of a double conforming decision (see c. 1644, §2; *DC*, art. 294). Furthermore, the extraordinary remedy of integral reinstatement (*restitutio in integrum*) is *ordinarily* not available in the case of a definitive sentence on marriage nullity because a case involving the status of persons, as stated earlier, does not become *res iudicata*. The recourse for a new hearing of the case, however, must be judged by the higher tribunal, that is, the Tribunal of the Roman Rota, and not by the local appeal tribunal, much less by the first instance tribunal (see c. 1644, §1; *DC,* art. 290, §1).

2 – Complaint of Nullity Against a Sentence

Is there a possibility for lodging a complaint of *irremediable* or *remediable* nullity against the double conforming sentence? If it is possible, which tribunal is competent to deal with such a complaint?

The law is clear about the possibility of irremediable or remediable nullity of judicial decisions, be they definitive or interlocutory. Canon 1620 (*DC*, art. 270) lists eight sources of *irremediable* nullity of a sentence and canon 1622 (*DC*, art. 272) identifies six instances in which a decision may be *remediably* null. In the case before us, three grounds of nullity are invoked in the complaints: violation of the right of defense (c. 1620, 7°; *DC*, art. 270, 7°), and absolute incompetence of the first instance judges (c. 1620, 1°; *DC*, art. 270, 1°), both constituting irremediable nullity; and illegitimate number of judges (c. 1622, 1°; *DC*, art. 272, 1°), resulting in remediable nullity.

According to canon 1621 (*DC*, art. 271), in a marriage nullity case a complaint of irremediable nullity against a definitive sentence can be proposed in perpetuity by way of an exception; by way of an action it can be proposed within ten years from the day the sentence is legitimately communicated to the parties. And in case of remediable nullity, the plaint must be proposed within three months from the notice of the publication of the sentence. In this case, once this three month period has elapsed, the sentence is considered to have been sanated *ipso iure* (see c. 1623; *DC*, art. 273).

Before whom should the complaint of nullity be presented? One must keep in mind the distinction to be made in this matter: the general principle is, when a complaint of nullity is proposed by way of an action, that is to say, independently of an appeal, it is to be decided by the judge who issued the sentence, unless the judge is considered suspect (see c. 1624; *DC*, art. 274, §1); for example, if the first instance judge has issued a sentence whose validity is now being challenged, it is the same judge who will deal with the matter, unless the judge is considered suspect. The same principle is applicable to a sentence of the second grade trial. If the validity of the second instance is challenged, it is the second instance judge who will deal with it.

The situation, however, is not the same if the validity of two or more sentences is challenged. If, for example, the validity of the decisions of first and second instance tribunals is called into question, then the plaint of nullity is to be handled by the court which issued the last sentence. Although the Code itself has no clear prescript on this situation, *DC*, article 274, §2 provides a clear norm on it: "If the complaint of nullity concerns sentences issued in two or more grades of trial, the judge who issued the last sentence is to hear the matter."[1] In other words, it is the judge of the second instance, and not that of the first instance, who is to determine the legitimacy of the complaint of nullity. The first instance judge is *absolutely incompetent* to judge this plaint of nullity.

The absolute incompetence of the first instance judge to deal with the complaint of nullity against decisions rendered in two or more instances is based on the following reasoning: When a case arrives at the appeal grade of trial, it must first cite the parties, or at least inform the parties of the fact of receipt of the *acta* together with the sentence, and invite them to submit any concerns or observations they may have about the case. Once the parties are *legitimately* cited or apprised of the status of the case, the appeal tribunal *alone* becomes competent to deal with that case in all its procedural aspects. The first instance tribunal is no longer competent by reason of grade of trial (and its incompetence over the case becomes *absolute*) to deal with any procedural aspects of the trial on which it has already pronounced its decision. This includes also any complaints of nullity against its own sentence. The first instance court, however, can certainly declare its own sentence null, either at the instance of the parties or of the defender of the bond, or *ex officio* before the case comes into the possession of the appeal court by *legitimate* citation. This principle has consequences for both the first instance court to judge the plaint of nullity and the participation of the defender of the bond of the first instance tribunal in the second grade of trial. In other words, the first instance tribunal has no legal relationship with the case and the defender of the bond of first instance has no *legitimacy* before the appeal court unless he or she has been appointed for the second grade of trial as well; but the defender of the bond of the first instance tribunal can certainly denounce the nullity of the sentences either directly to the second instance tribunal or through its defender of the bond or promoter of justice, which could then deal with the complaint *ex officio*.

3 – Consequences of Using an Illegitimate Number of Judges

---

[1] Klaus Lüdicke and Ronny E. Jenkins, *Dignitas Connubii: Norms and Commentary* (Washington, DC: Canon Law Society of America, 2006), 445.

It is alleged in this case that the decree declaring the nullity of both sentences was issued by a single substitute judge of the first instance, whereas the first instance sentence itself was rendered by a college of three judges. Therefore, the advocate of the petitioner argued that the decree was remediably null because it was rendered by an illegitimate number of judges contrary to the explicit requirement of law. The law states that a sentence issued by an illegitimate number of judges contrary to the prescript of canon 1441 (*DC*, art. 30, §1) is remediably null (see c. 1441; c. 1622, 1°; *DC*, art. 272, 1°). That is to say, a case judged by a collegiate tribunal in first instance must be judged by the tribunal of second instance consisting of the same number of judges, and this requirement is for the validity of the sentence.

It was argued in this case that it was legitimate for a single judge to decree the nullity of the sentences, and this view was based on the opinion of Antoni Stankiewicz, the present Dean of the Roman Rota and without doubt one of the renowned jurists of our time, in his commentary on canon 1627. Stankiewicz said the following in his commentary on the canon, prior to the promulgation of *DC*:

> Although, in cases of matrimonial nullity, the judgment is pronounced by a collegiate tribunal (c. 1425, § 1, 1° b), the plaint of nullity against these judgments can be heard by a sole judge, since the special norm for oral process so allows (cc. 1657, 1441). However, the sole judge may use two assessors (c. 1424), and if the issue of nullity presents any particular difficulty to resolve, a collegiate tribunal can judge it (see c. 1425, § 2).[2]

In the above statement, Stankiewicz cites canons 1657 and 1441 in support of his view that a plaint of nullity against the decisions in marriage nullity cases can be heard by a single judge court. In the source cited (i.e., the *Exegetical Commentary*), it is not Stankiewicz who comments on canon 1657, but Luis Madero, who says:

> However, it is convenient to bear in mind that, in some cases, the competent judge, in order to hear a case in accord with the oral contentious process, will not be the judge of first instance, since one must consider other criteria regarding competence. Consider, for example, the plaint of nullity of the sentence when it has been pronounced by a collegial tribunal. This collegial tribunal would

---

[2] Antoni Stankiewicz, Commentary on Canon 1627, in *Exegetical Commentary on the Code of Canon Law*, eds. Ángel Marzoa, Jorge Miras, and Rafael Rodríguez-Ocaña (Montréal, Canada: Wilson & Lafleur, 2004), IV/2:1565.

> have to be the same tribunal that would have to resolve the plaint in accordance with c. 1624.[3]

In essence, according to Madero, a plaint of nullity must be judged by the same college (number) of judges who pronounced the sentence. The plaint of nullity cannot be decided by a single judge court.

This is the meaning conveyed in his commentary on canon 1657 by John Beal in the *New Commentary on the Code of Canon Law*. Beal says:

> A collegiate tribunal is necessary at any grade of trial for the judicial resolution of incidental cases when the principal case has been entrusted to a college (c. 1590, §1) and for the resolution of complaints of nullity when the impugned sentence has been issued by a college (c. 1624). The Roman Rota always proceeds collegially regardless of the process used.[4]

In fact, in support of this view, Beal cites Stankiewicz's article of 1992 published in *Apollinaris*.[5] Although Stankiewicz enjoys enormous academic credibility because of his unique contribution to numerous issues of canonical science, his view on this particular matter does not seem tenable. This is more so because of what *DC* has to say on the issue.

Article 6 of *DC*, reiterating the prescript of canon 1690 of the Code, says that causes for the declaration of nullity of marriage cannot be handled through the oral process. And article 269 rules that if the appeal tribunal discovers that the oral contentious process was used in the lower grade of trial, it is to declare the nullity of the sentence and remit the cause to the tribunal which issued the sentence. This is the application of the general norm applicable to any contentious trial. But in its article 277, §1, *DC* permits the processing of a complaint of nullity against a decision through oral contentious process under certain conditions. But in the second paragraph of the same article, *DC* stipulates: "It pertains, however, to a collegial tribunal to hear the nullity of a decision issued by a collegial tribunal." Therefore, it should be clear to any reader that a plaint of nullity against a decision pronounced by a college of

---

[3] Luis Madero, Commentary on Canon, 1657, in *Exegetical Commentary on the Code of Canon Law*, eds. Ángel Marzoa, Jorge Miras, and Rafael Rodríguez-Ocaña (Montréal, Canada: Wilson & Lafleur, 2004), IV/2: 1691-1692. According to Zenon Grocholewski, "Infatti nessuna delle cause riservate al tribunale collegiale (can. 1425, §1) può essere trattata col processo orale." See Zenon Grocholewski, Commentary on Canon 1657, in *Commento al Codice di diritto canonico*, 2nd ed. (Città del Vaticano: Libreria editrice Vaticana, 2001), 955.

[4] John P. Beal, Commentary on Canon 1657, in *New Commentary on the Code of Canon Law*, eds. John P. Beal, James A. Coriden, and Thomas J. Green (New York, NY: Paulist Press, 2000), 1755.

[5] See Antoni Stankiewicz, "Il processo contenzioso orale," *Apollinaris* 64 (1992) 583.

judges must be judged by a collegiate tribunal and not by a single judge court. In fact, this principle is not a creation of *DC*, but it was already present in doctrine and jurisprudence, now clearly stated in *DC*, article 277, §2.

In light of this discussion, we must conclude with regard to the proper manner of proceeding in the case of a plaint of nullity against a sentence issued by a collegiate tribunal, that it must be judged by a collegiate panel (*DC*, art. 277, §2), and not by a single judge; any decision contrary to this prescript would be *remediably* null in accord with the norm of *DC*, article 272, 1° (c. 1622, 1°). This decision is subject to appeal (*DC*, art. 277, §3) all the way to the Roman Rota.

In light of these observations, the following conclusions could be proposed in this case:

First, *the defender of the bond of first instance lodged a plaint of irremediable nullity against the first instance sentence*—The defender of the bond of first instance lacked the *legitimacy* to present the plaint of nullity to the first instance tribunal directly. He could have advised the respondent to lodge the plaint of nullity personally before the appeal court or he could have done so *indirectly*, that is, either through the defender of the bond or promoter of justice of the second instance, or by denouncing the nullity to the appeal court. In any case, it was the tribunal of appeal that was competent to deal with the plaint of nullity of both, first and second instance, decisions.

Second, *the sole judge of first instance declared the first instance sentence and the subsequent decree of confirmation irremediably null on the ground of violation of the respondent's right of defence*—although it was quite possible that the respondent's right of defence was violated, the first instance tribunal was *absolutely incompetent* to judge the plaint of nullity against the two first round definitive decisions for *reason of grade of trial*. The challenge against the decisions should have been brought before the appeal tribunal, which alone was competent to adjudicate it at the local level, or before the Roman Rota.

Third, *the petitioner's advocate lodged a plaint of remediable nullity against the decree declaring the two original sentences irremediably null on the ground that the decision was not rendered by the college of judges but by the sole substitute judge and that the same decision was not pronounced by the original judge*—From the preceding conclusion what follows can be regarded as irrelevant or moot, nevertheless it is important to note that the nullity of the decree of the sole judge declaring the irremediable nullity of the two preceding definitive decisions was alleged on the principle that it was issued contrary to the prescript of canon 1441 (*DC*, art. 30, §4), and consequently, it was *remediably* null in accord with the norm of canon 1622, 1° (*DC*, art. 272, 1°).

Thus, in summary: The decree of the sole judge declaring the irremediable nullity of the two preceding definitive decisions was itself null on two grounds: a) *absolute incompetence*, because the plaint of nullity should have been judged by the appeal court. In light of canon 1620, 1° (*DC*, art. 270, 1°), therefore, the decree was *irremediably null*; and b) for lack of legitimate number of judges in issuing the decision on the plaint of nullity; therefore, it was *remediably* null in accord with the prescript of canon 1622, 1° (*DC*, art. 272, 1°). In light of the preceding ground of *irremediable* nullity of the decree, the second one is indeed juridically irrelevant or moot.

Because the decree was *irremediably* null, the introduction of the case in the second round before the first instance tribunal is to be considered *non-existent*. This is so because of two conforming decisions which had already declared the marriage null. Therefore, there was no cause for reintroduction, because there was no juridically valid marriage to be impugned. It was *res quasi iudicata*. In other words, the action of the first instance introducing the case which had become *res quasi iudicata* amounted to judging a juridically non-existent marriage because by two affirmative decisions the marriage had been declared invalid. The plaint of nullity should have been judged by the second (appeal) instance tribunal or it should have been referred to the Roman Rota. Furthermore, any decision of the appeal tribunal is subject to appeal before the Roman Rota and not before the Supreme Tribunal of the Apostolic Signatura.

Rev. Augustine Mendonça, J.C.D.

CANON 1641

RES IUDICATA WITHOUT CONCORDANT SENTENCES IN *GRAVIORA DELICTA* CASES

*It appears that if there is an appeal in a judicial trial of a case involving a more grave delict (*delictum gravius*) the decision of the second instance tribunal is the final one, even if it reverses the first instance decision. Is this true? How does this practice fit with the general norms of the contentious process requiring two concordant sentences?*

OPINION

To see this question in proper context, we need to look at how a case arrives at *res iudicata*. Of course, we need to keep in mind that criminal cases are not cases involving the status of persons. Rather, they determine whether or not an ecclesiastical crime has been committed and, if so, what penalty is to be issued. Although the penalty itself would certainly affect the status of a priest or deacon in these cases, the juridic question settled by the tribunal is not directly the status of the cleric.

Simply comparing the text of the 2001 *motu proprio Sacramentorum Sanctitatis Tutela* (*SST*) about *res iudicata* with what the 1983 *Code of Canon Law* states reveals the marked difference between the two laws:

***SST*, Article 23, 1°**[1]	**Canon 1641, 1°**
Res iudicata habetur:	*Firmo praescripto can. 1643, res iudicata habetur:*
1° *Si sententia in secunda instantia prolata fuerit;*	1° *si duplex intercesserit inter easdem partes sententia conformis de eodem petito et ex eadem causa petendi;*
A *res iudicata* occurs:	Without prejudice to the prescript of can. 1643, a *res iudicata* occurs:
1° if a sentence has been rendered in second instance;	1° if a second concordant sentence is rendered between the same parties over the same issue and on the same cause for petitioning;

[1] Pope John Paul II, *motu proprio Sacramentorum Sanctitatis Tutela*, April 30, 2001, *Acta Apostolicae Sedis* 93 (2001) 737-739; trans. Gregory Ingels, revised by Joseph R. Punderson and Charles J. Scicluna in "A Resource for Canonical Processes for the Resolution of Complaints of Clerical Sexual Abuse of Minors" (Unpublished), November 2003, 34.

According to canon 1641, 1°, a twofold conforming sentence is required before a sentence can be *res iudicata*. It is clear that *SST*, article 23, 1° does not mention the requirement of the twofold conforming sentence. Therefore, in cases that are adjudicated under the provisions of *SST*, there is no requirement of the twofold conforming sentence. Thus, for example, although the first instance sentence declared that the accused was guilty and, therefore, incurred the penalty of dismissal from the clerical state, the second instance sentence might reach a sentence of *non constat*. This second sentence would stand and become a *res iudicata*.

In order to understand article 23 of *SST*, we need to look at canon 1629, 1°, which states that "There is no appeal ... from a sentence of the Supreme Pontiff himself or the Apostolic Signatura." There is an important commentary on this canon in the *Exegetical Commentary on the Code of Canon Law* by Paulo Moneta.[2] The author makes reference to canon 1405, §1, 4°, which states:

> It is solely the right of the Roman Pontiff himself to judge in the cases mentioned in canon 1401 *[namely, all cases for which the Church claims competence by proper and exclusive right]*: ... other cases which he has called to his own judgment.

Moneta notes that the Holy Father usually does not directly exercise his judicial power, but usually requests one of the Apostolic Tribunals to handle the case by his special commission. Although the judgments in these cases are normally subject to appeal as well as the principle of the twofold conforming sentence, the Holy Father may include a clause which precludes an appeal (*appellatio remota*).

It appears that Moneta's analysis applies to these cases of grave delicts. *SST*, article 6, §1 explicitly indicates that "The Congregation for the Doctrine of the Faith is the Supreme Apostolic Tribunal ... for the judgment of delicts defined in the preceding articles." In other words, the judicial function of the Roman Pontiff in these cases is exercised by the Congregation. *SST*, article 23, moreover, provides for appeal, up to second instance. It states, "A *res iudicata* occurs if a sentence has been rendered in second instance" (1°). Beyond that, it is not able to be appealed. The basis for the limit is additionally expressed in *SST*, article 6, §3, which states: "The sentences of this Supreme Tribunal (*of*

---

[2] See Paolo Moneta, Commentary on Canon 1629, in *Exegetical Commentary on the Code of Canon Law*, eds. Ángel Marzoa, Jorge Miras, and Rafael Rodríguez-Ocaña (Montréal: Wilson & Lafleur, 2004), IV/2:1570.

the Congregation for the Doctrine of the Faith), rendered within the limits of its proper competence, do not need to be submitted for thc approval of the Supreme Pontiff."

The combination of *SST*, articles 6, §3 and 23 makes perfect sense in view of the norm of canon 1629, 1°: "There is no appeal … from a sentence of the Supreme Pontiff himself or the Apostolic Signatura." In regard to these cases, the Congregation in second instance is like the Apostolic Signatura. Once it is decided, it is final (*res iudicata*). Note the full title *Supreme Tribunal of the Apostolic Signatura* and the full title "The Congregation for the Doctrine of the Faith is the Supreme Apostolic Tribunal … for the judgment of the delict…." As a supreme court, there must be an instance at which the case ends, whether it confirms or overturns the decision of a lower court.

Thus, these authors are of the opinion that it would be better to say that *SST,* article 23 is not so much a divergence from the general law, as it is a particular specification of the general law concerning the exercise of the judicial function of the Roman Pontiff. Nevertheless, depending on the judgment of second instance, this norm can allow for reaching *res iudicata* without having *duplex conformis sententia.*

Rev. Msgr. Mark L. Bartchak, J.C.D.
Rev. Msgr. Frederick C. Easton, J.C.L.

CANON 1673, 3º

COMPETENCE OF THE TRIBUNAL OF THE PETITIONER'S DOMICILE WHEN THE RESPONDENT'S WHEREABOUTS ARE UNKNOWN

With some frequency our tribunal is approached by parties who were married outside of the diocese, whose witnesses are scattered throughout the country, and whose former spouses' whereabouts are unknown. The common practice since the promulgation of the 1983 Code of Canon Law has been for the tribunal to "exempt itself" from the conditions established in canon 1673, 3º. Is this a licit practice?

OPINION

To the regular reader of *CLSA Advisory Opinions*, the present question will seem quite familiar since it has been previously addressed by several canonists.[1] The present opinion is not redundant, however, since it aims to propose a basis for an opposing view. After presenting my own argument, I intend to respond in turn to the opposing arguments.

The conditions of canon 1673, 3º are imposed by the law and cannot be omitted even in the scenario presented.[2] As the January 25, 2005 Instruction of the Pontifical Council for Legislative Texts, *Dignitas Connubii,* says, until these conditions "have been fulfilled, the tribunal cannot proceed legitimately" (art. 13, §1).[3] This norm could have easily addressed the specific scenario in question, which has been debated by canonists for over two decades. Indeed, on other occasions the Instruction establishes norms for particular situations that have arisen in tribunals since the promulgation of the Code (e.g., arts. 56,

---

[1] James H. Provost, "Canon 1673," *Roman Replies and CLSA Advisory Opinions 1984*, eds. William A. Schumacher and Richard A Hill, S.J. (Washington, DC: Canon Law Society of America, 1984), 61-63; John B. Hesch, "Competence of Tribunal When Respondent's Whereabouts Remain Unknown," and Michael Manzelli, "Competence of Tribunals With Unlocatable Respondents," *CLSA Advisory Opinions 1994-2000*, ed. Arthur J. Espelage, O.F.M. (Washington, DC: Canon Law Society of America, 2002), 498-503 and 510-511, respectively; Augustine Mendonça, "Tribunal Competence When Respondent's Whereabouts Are Unknown," *Roman Replies and CLSA Advisory Opinions 2004*, eds. F. Stephen Pedone and James I. Donlon (Alexandria, VA: Canon Law Society of America, 2004), 181-188.

[2] Among the authors who share this view are Eduardo Baura, "La funzione di vigilanza sulla retta amministrazione della giustizia," *Ius Ecclesiae* 6 (1994) 356-357; Joaquín Llobell, "Article 1 The Competent Forum," in *Exegetical Commentary on the Code of Canon Law*, eds. Ángel Marzoa, Jorge Miras, and Rafael Rodríguez-Ocaña (Montréal: Wilson & Lafleur, 2004), IV/2:1771.

[3] Klaus Lüdicke and Ronny E. Jenkins, *Dignitas Connubii: Norms and Commentary* (Washington, DC: Canon Law Society of America, 2006), 42.

§§5-6; 101; 258); but it saw fit simply to reiterate the conditions established in canon 1673, 3° without allowing tribunals to exempt themselves from them when a respondent cannot be located.

Likewise, a decree of the Supreme Tribunal of the Apostolic Signatura states: "... the tribunal of the place in which the petitioner has a domicile is not the forum that is competent by law for handling a cause of marriage nullity, unless the conditions mentioned in c. 1673, 3° are truly verified, namely, 'provided that both parties reside in the territory of the same conference of bishops, and the judicial vicar of the respondent's domicile consents after hearing the party.'"[4] Again, no exceptions are indicated; without the fulfillment of the conditions, the tribunal remains relatively incompetent.

Returning to the pertinent legislation (*lex*) itself, as even many of the authors cited above note, canon 1673, 3° constitutes an exception in the law. The general principle regarding competence is *actor sequitur forum rei* ("the petitioner follows the forum of the defendant"), and this principle is articulated in canon 1407, §3: "*Actor sequitur forum partis conventae.*" Adjudicating a cause in the forum of the petitioner, therefore, is an exception to this principle, an exception which is received in the law in two places relevant to our discussion. First, for trials in general, when a person's domicile, quasi-domicile and place of residence are unknown, the petitioner's tribunal is competent "provided that no other legitimate forum is available" (c. 1409, §2). If another forum is available, the petitioner's forum is not competent. The second exception here is canon 1673, 3°. As exceptions in the law, these canons are to be read strictly: "Laws which ... contain an exception from the law are subject to strict interpretation" (c. 18). All of the conditions contained in this exception, therefore, must be observed, unless a particular favor is granted by the Apostolic Signatura in accord with its competence (see *Pastor Bonus*, art. 124, 2°-3°).

It can happen that, indeed, no other competent tribunal is available to handle the petitioner's cause of marriage nullity; in such a case, one can rely on canon 1409, §2. For instance, if the respondent's whereabouts are unknown, the proofs are scattered throughout different dioceses, and the

---

[4] Supreme Tribunal of the Apostolic Signatura, *Responsio per generale decretum ad propositum quæsitum de can. 1673, 3° C.I.C.*, May 6, 1993, Prot. No. 23192/92 VT, *Acta Apostolicae Sedis* 85 (1993) 969; trans. William L. Daniel: "... *tribunal loci in quo pars actrix domicilium habet non est forum iure competens ad pertractandam causam nullitatis matrimonii, nisi reapse verificentur conditiones de quibus in can. 1673, 3°, scilicet 'dummodo utraque pars in territorio eiusdem Episcoporum Conferentiæ degat, et Vicarius iudicialis domicilii partis conventæ, ipsa audita, consentiat.'*"

tribunal of the place of the celebration is truly unavailable (e.g., there is no functioning tribunal, the tribunal is closed for six months due to damage of the building and equipment, the petitioner does not speak the same language as the tribunal personnel), then the principle often cited can be applied: "*Nemo potest ad impossibile obligari*" (*Regula Juris* 6 in VI°). That is, if it is impossible for the petitioner to exercise his right in any other way, then the tribunal of the petitioner's domicile can handle the case licitly. If one is hesitant, the problem could be referred to the Apostolic Signatura.

The principal arguments in favor of the self-exemption of the conditions of canon 1673, 3° by tribunals are especially the following eight:

1. The key document upon which the cited canonists base their arguments is a rescript of the Apostolic Signatura dated April 6, 1973.[5] A diocesan tribunal had asked the Supreme Tribunal if it could handle a cause of marriage nullity since a majority of the proofs were found in the territory of the diocese, even though the respondent's whereabouts were unknown. This title of competence was established in Pope Paul VI's *motu proprio* of March 28, 1971, *Causas matrimoniales*, the *ius vigens* at the time in this matter.[6] The Apostolic Signatura stated that the tribunal was competent to handle the case even without a prorogation of competence, since the cited norm is directed especially toward a simpler and more rapid instruction of the cause.

The cited canonists hold that this piece of jurisprudence may be applied to canon 1673, 3° and that canon 1673, 3° is also directed toward ease of instruction. In the first place, there is no doubt that the cited norm of *Causas matrimoniales* is abrogated (c. 6, §1, 4°). Its value for understanding the current law, beyond being a legislative source, lies in the specific matters that it addresses. The cited norm addresses only the forum of the majority of the proofs, not the forum of the petitioner's domicile; it therefore remains useful in the application of canon 1673, 4°, and indeed the aim of this law is much the same as the cited 1971 norm: when the majority of the proofs of a cause are present in a given territory (i.e., the witnesses of both parties, any documents

---

[5] Provost provides an unofficial translation of this rescript at the end of his opinion cited in note 1 above.

[6] See Pope Paul VI, Apostolic Letter *motu proprio*, *Causas matrimoniales*, March 28, 1971, Art. IV, §1 c), *Acta Apostolicae Sedis* 63 (1971) 443. The norm states that, among others, the tribunal competent to adjudicate the cause is "the tribunal of the place in which a majority of the depositions or proofs are in fact to be collected, provided that the ordinary of the place of the respondent's habitual residence and the local ordinary and presiding judge of the tribunal approached consents"; trans. William L. Daniel.

attainable there, etc.), the case is perhaps best adjudicated there. The aim of canon 1673, 3° is quite distinct from this, however.

The prevalent value of canon 1673, 3° is not the facilitation of a rapid instruction of the cause but the protection of the respondent's right of defense. Indeed, this is evident both in jurisprudence and law (*ius*). In 1993, the Apostolic Signatura issued a general administrative decree regarding the correct application of canon 1673, 3°.[7] In that document, the Dicastery emphasizes the right of defense by referring itself to a previous document where it states the following:

> In order for him to grant or deny consent, the judicial vicar of the respondent's domicile must especially weigh the respondent's difficulties in defending himself before the other tribunal, for example, due to a difference of language, great distance, etc. The right of defense does not only require that the party be heard, but also that he in fact have the opportunity to know the petitions, the proofs, and the deductions brought forward by the other party or *ex officio*, and to challenge them appropriately...[8]

In addition, *Dignitas Connubii,* article 13, §4, states the following regarding the observance of the conditions found in canon 1673, 3°: "Before giving his consent, the Judicial Vicar of the domicile of the respondent party is to consider carefully all the circumstances of the cause, especially the difficulties of the respondent party in defending himself before the tribunal of the place in which the petitioning party has a domicile or in which the greater part of the proofs are to be collected."[9] The previous consultation with the respondent and his judicial vicar seems to be chiefly (if not exclusively) directed toward safeguarding the respondent's right of defense. The Apostolic Signatura's explanation from the 1973 rescript, therefore, cannot be imposed on canon 1673, 3°.

---

[7] Supreme Tribunal of the Apostolic Signatura, "*Considerata quoque declaratione huius Signaturæ Apostolicæ diei 27 Aprilis 1989, n. 4,*" *Acta Apostolicae Sedis* 85 (1993) 970.

[8] Supreme Tribunal of the Apostolic Signatura, *Declaratio de foro plerarumque probationum*, April 27, 1989, Prot. no. 20681/89 VT, no. 4, in *Communicationes* 21 (1989) 115-116; trans. William L. Daniel: "*Vicarius iudicialis domicilii partis conventæ, in ordine ad consensum præstandum vel minus, præsertim perpendere debet difficultates partis conventæ sese defendendi coram illo tribunali, v.g. ob diversitatem linguæ, magnam distantiam, etc. Ius defensionis non tantum requirit ut audiatur pars, verum etiam ut ipsa, si velit, de facto petitiones, probationes, et deductiones sive ab altera parte sive ex officio allatas cognoscere et iisdem apte contradicere possit.*"

[9] Klaus Lüdicke and Ronny E. Jenkins, *Dignitas Connubii: Norms and Commentary*, 42-43.

2. One author refers at length to a 1993 rescript of the Apostolic Signatura granting competence to a tribunal of the petitioner's domicile when the respondent's whereabouts were unknown.[10] The author states that the 1993 rescript confirmed the principles found in the 1973 rescript since both did not object to the handling of the cause by the tribunal of the petitioner's domicile. The 1993 rescript, however, in no way implies that tribunals have a right to exempt themselves from the conditions in canon 1673, 3º. In the request for the prorogation of competence, the petitioning judicial vicar expressly asked the following at the end of his letter: "Further, in the future where it has been determined after a mature and diligent investigation that it is morally impossible to locate the respondent, I ask whether it is always necessary to seek the permission of the Apostolic Signatura before proceeding to accept a libellus and to base competency on canon 1673, 3º?" While the Apostolic Signatura granted the prorogation, it notably omitted an affirmative response to this question; presumably, therefore, the specific conditions established in the law should be followed if one does not obtain a prorogation from the Supreme Tribunal. The 1993 response is markedly different from that of 1973. In the latter, the petitioning judicial vicar did not ask if the prorogation of the Apostolic Signatura was needed when the respondent could not be found, and the Apostolic Signatura *ex officio* stated that prorogation was unnecessary. In the 1993 rescript, the Apostolic Signatura had an open opportunity to recall the jurisprudence found in the 1973 rescript, but it deemed it unsuitable to refer to it. Finally, there is a very significant juridical difference between the 1973 rescript and the 1993 rescript. While the former stated that no grant was needed, the latter indicates that a grant *is* needed and, in fact, it granted the prorogation. Such a grant would have been superfluous if judicial vicars had the liberty to exempt themselves from the conditions of canon 1673, 3º when the respondent cannot be found.

3. One of the cited canonists maintains that, since canon 1673 does not deal with the situation in which a respondent's whereabouts are unknown, there is a *lacuna* in the law, and therefore one must rely on sources not found in the law or legitimate custom (c. 19). In my view, this is a hasty invocation of canon 19, since the law does not fail to consider this situation; rather it

---

[10] Mendonça, 184-187; For the text of the 1993 rescript, see Supreme Tribunal of the Apostolic Signatura, "Canon 1673. Competence," November 15, 1993, in *Roman Replies and CLSA Advisory Opinions 1994*, eds. Kevin W. Vann and James I. Donlon (Washington, DC: Canon Law Society of America, 1994), 54-59.

imposes conditions on the licit handling of a cause by the petitioner's tribunal. The legislator is not inclined to provide exceptions to the conditions in canon 1673, 3º, because he does not deem the petitioner's tribunal the opportune forum without a prior consultation of the respondent and his judicial vicar. Since the law provides for the situation it wishes to address, the supposed *lacuna* does not exist.[11]

4. When advancing their view, not a few canonists cite the rule of law, "*Nemo potest ad impossibile obligari*" (*Regula Juris* 6 in VIº), thereby indicating that, if it is impossible to locate the respondent, the conditions established do not apply. This position presumes that the legislator equally favors all of the *fora* indicated in canon 1673 and that the petitioner has a right to have his cause judged at his local tribunal. This cannot be maintained, however, insofar as the tribunal of the place of the celebration and the tribunal of the respondent's domicile or quasi-domicile (c. 1673, 1º-2º) are available to the petitioner without any conditions; these two *fora* are legitimate *sic et simpliciter* without any exceptions, and the petitioner has a clear right to have his cause judged before them. The petitioner has a right to have his cause judged before the other two *fora* (c. 1673, 3º-4º) *if certain conditions are fulfilled*. The legislator intends to impose these conditions; if it is impossible to fulfill them, then these *fora* are unavailable to the petitioner. Since North American petitioners usually have several options, *Regula Iuris* 6 should not be invoked until it actually becomes impossible for them to pursue their cause at another legitimate tribunal (c. 1409, §2).

5. The cited canonists justifiably insist on the petitioner's right to present a petition accusing his marriage of nullity (c. 1674, 1º). This right, however, is not exempt from certain regulations (c. 1505, §2). If the approached tribunal is incompetent (e.g., if the tribunal of his domicile cannot acquire the consent of the judicial vicar of the respondent's domicile because the latter's whereabouts are unknown), then the petitioner cannot insist that his cause be judged there

---

[11] In this author's opinion, the longstanding tribunal practice of overlooking the conditions in c. 1673, 3º in the scenario being considered is the early stage of the formulation of a custom contrary to the law; and the Signatura has never explicitly forbidden the practice in a widespread way. Since it cannot have been observed yet for thirty years–having taken effect in 1983–it does not yet enjoy the force of law (c. 23). Though I have not seen the argument made, one might base the practice of self-exemption from these conditions on c. 27, the principle that custom is the best interpreter of the law. In my opinion, however, the law is clear, and the practice being disputed is not an interpretation of c. 1673, 3º, but an innovation that is in tension with evident conditions established in the law.

(c. 1505, §2, 1°). The petitioner has a right to present his case, not to have the forum of his choice contrary to the norm of law.

6. The cited canonists assert that referring the petitioner to the place of the celebration (c. 1673, 1°) can often be unjust since this inconveniences the party for no good reason; the tribunal may be 1,000 miles away and the party may have no actual connection to that place. This argument, however, is for the most part unrealistic for two reasons: Firstly, most of the party's contact with the tribunal is done by means of the mail system (e.g., exchange of documents, letters, etc.) and modern means of communication (e.g., telephone, e-mail). No matter where one is, it is relatively convenient to participate in a marriage nullity trial. Secondly, the main personal contact the petitioner has with the tribunal is his deposition with an auditor; when a person's cause is handled by a distant tribunal, this auditor is usually an auditor of the tribunal of the petitioner's domicile anyway (c. 1418). All things considered, therefore, the petitioner's experience may be exactly the same regardless of which tribunal handles his cause. If the practices of the tribunal of the place of the celebration render the petitioner's involvement unduly cumbersome, one could begin to question whether that tribunal is actually available to him (c. 1409, §2).

7. One canonist argues that reliance on canon 1418 is insufficient, because then "the moral certitude in the minds of the judges will have to remain based upon an evaluation *super actis*." This statement is astounding since the legislator in facts *insists* that the moral certitude of the judges be based *solely* on the contents of the acts (see cc. 1608, §2 and 1604, §1.).

8. Finally, several canonists state that a non-observance of the conditions contained in canon 1673, 3° does not make the sentence null, and therefore they can be ignored in certain cases. Aside from the fact that this is an implicit acknowledgement that the tribunal's handling of the cause is illicit, this minimalistic approach to the law should be avoided. The laws of the Church (albeit not beyond the need for continual legislative reform) are directed toward the eternal and juridical (*iura*) good of the people of God and those attached to them in some way. These ends are harmed if one willingly excuses himself from observing certain laws merely because they are not imposed under pain of invalidity.

William L. Daniel, J.C.L.

CANON 1684, §1

LIFTING A *MONITUM* ATTACHED TO A SENTENCE

A couple in my parish wishes to marry in the Church. The gentleman received an annulment of his first marriage. The presiding judge attached a monitum *to the declaration of nullity. The conditions in the* monitum *have been fulfilled over a period of many years and a report was sent to the tribunal as required. Because this is not a* vetitum, *I understood that, as pastor, I can determine whether the concerns raised by the judge have been properly addressed as part of the marriage preparation. However, the new judicial vicar of the diocese has recently added further requirements, indicating that the parties are not ready for marriage in the Church because the man might lapse into his old, destructive behavior. We are at an impasse. May I witness the marriage of this couple?*

OPINION

The canonical character of a *vetitum* arises from canons 1684 and 1685 of the Code of Canon Law. A *vetitum* attached to the declaration of nullity prohibits a new marriage until the tribunal that issued the sentence has been consulted. A *vetitum* is to be added to the sentence of nullity if the party was found to be absolutely impotent or incapable of marriage by reason of a permanent incapacity (see *Dignitas Connubii*, art. 251, §1). This prohibition is employed when the issues are so grave that the party may not be able to enter into a valid marriage. A *vetitum* is not an invalidating impediment to marriage unless the supreme authority of the Church has added such a nullifying clause (c. 1077, §2).

A *monitum*, on the other hand, is not found in the Code of Canon Law. It is a custom that has arisen among some tribunals to warn the parties and the pastoral minister who assists at the new marriage that certain conditions should be fulfilled before the marriage is celebrated. In the opinion of the tribunal, the one who received the annulment has issues that might cause the invalidity of a new marriage. A *monitum* is not an invalidating obstacle to a future marriage.

Because a *monitum* is not an institute of law, the universal law of the Church does not regulate its issuance or specify how it is to be satisfied. The diocese may issue guidelines or directives concerning the procedure for lifting this injunction.

As the words themselves indicate, a *vetitum* is a prohibition; a *monitum* is a warning. A *vetitum* prohibits a future marriage because it is judged that the marriage would be invalid. A *monitum* warns that one or both parties of the annulled marriage need special attention and preparation in order that a future marriage be both valid and successful.

It is the responsibility of the pastor to ensure that the couple is properly prepared for marriage. The issues that were mentioned in the *monitum* are to be addressed as part of the appropriate preparations for marriage as required by law (c. 1063, 2°). The directives of the diocese might well require that the pastor report to the tribunal what steps were taken to remove any obstacles to a successful marriage and include the pastor's judgment as to the preparedness of the parties for marriage. In my opinion, the pastor has the final decision as to the preparedness of such a couple.

This couple is free to marry in the Church and marriage is one of the fundamental natural human rights. All laws and directives that restrict this freedom are subject to strict interpretation (c. 18). It is my opinion that you may proceed to witness this marriage.

You indicate that your judgment on the preparedness of this couple is at odds with the opinion of the judicial vicar. You might wish to take this case directly to the diocesan bishop. You would not be asking the bishop for his approval of your judgment or to make his own the determination of the readiness of the couple to marry. It would be to inform him of the conflict that has arisen and to give the bishop prior notice of your decision to witness this marriage.

Rev. Paul L. Golden, C.M., J.C.D.

CANON 517, §2 (*CCEO*)

MARONITE NOVICE IN A LATIN CHURCH RELIGIOUS INSTITUTE

I am the major superior of a Latin Church religious institute of diocesan right. Most of the sisters in this congregation are teachers or administrators. After completing our admission requirements, a Maronite Catholic woman in good standing with the Catholic Church began the year of candidacy. She was then admitted into the two-year novitiate. After finishing the canonical year, she began experiencing the works of this institute during her second year. In a few months, that year will end. I anticipate that the sister will be accepted for first profession in accordance with our constitution and statutes. Since she is a Maronite Catholic, is anything else required?

OPINION

There are twenty-two *sui iuris* Churches in the Catholic Church. The Latin Church is one of them. The other twenty-one are Eastern Catholic Churches.[1] The term *sui iuris* is often translated as "self-governing" or "autonomous." While these autonomous Churches "are of equal rank, so that none of them is superior to the others because of its rite," they "are none the less equally entrusted to the pastoral guidance of the Roman Pontiff, who by God's appointment is successor to Blessed Peter in primacy over the Universal Church."[2]

Since the woman is a Maronite Catholic, the *Code of Canons of the Eastern Churches* (*CCEO*) binds her. That Code contains more impediments than the ones listed in the *Code of Canon Law* for admission to religious institutes. From our conversation, it appears that this woman does not have any of those impediments. Additionally, canon 517, §2 of the *CCEO* says, "No one is admitted lawfully (*licite*) to the novitiate of a religious institute of another Church *sui iuris* without the permission (*licentia*) of the Apostolic See, unless it is a candidate who is destined for a province or house, mentioned in can. 432, of his own Church."

---

[1] Appendix V in *Comparative Sacramental Discipline in the CCEO and CIC*, ed. Francis J. Marini (Washington, DC: Canon Law Society of America, 2003), 255-258.

[2] Second Vatican Council, "Decree on the Catholic Eastern Churches," *Orientalium Ecclesiarum*, November 21, 1964, no. 3, *Acta Apostolicae Sedis* 57 (1965); English translation from *Vatican II: The Conciliar and Post Conciliar Documents*, ed. Austin Flannery, O.P. (Collegeville, MN: The Liturgical Press, 1992), 442.

On the surface, it might seem that this canon pertains only to Eastern Catholic Churches. If that were true then it would only apply to a Maronite woman seeking admission into a Ukranian religious institute, for example. However, canon 1 moderates the absolute character of the *CCEO* by establishing its relationship with the Latin Church. Such a concept is not surprising since both Codes are the framework for canon law within the Catholic Church. Furthermore, even though there is no explicit mention of the Latin Church in canon 517, it was in the mind of the *Coetus de monachis* when it drafted the 1979 Provisional Schema.[3]

The canon itself requires the permission (*licentia*) of the Apostolic See for an Eastern Church Catholic for admittance into the novitiate. The Apostolic Constitution *Pastor Bonus* grants this competence to the Congregation for the Oriental Churches (art. 58, §1). The Congregation gives permission by way of an indult of accommodation. This enables the individual to conform in every way to the rite observed by the religious institute. A change of rite is not required. The individual remains ascribed to her or his own rite.[4] As indicated in the canon, this matter does not pertain if the same candidate is intended for a house or province of his or her own Church *sui iuris*.

Having given service to religious congregations in such matters on a variety of occasions, and having reviewed the responses from the Congregation for the Oriental Churches, I would recommend that you do the following in this situation: The novice needs an understanding of the basic concepts pertaining to this matter. Once she comprehends them, she should compose a petition to the Congregation requesting regularization of her status and an indult of accommodation. Incorporating her baptismal name, as well as her religious name, she should also describe her calling to this particular institute. A baptismal certificate should be included. The petition should also include a letter from you as superior of the institute.

Since her novitiate is valid but illicit, your letter can state that it recently came to your attention that the Holy See requires a special permission to be obtained before admitting the individual into the novitiate. Indicate that the novice understands the issues, and that you are supporting her request for regularization of her status and the indult of accommodation. Furthermore,

---

[3] Jobe Abbass, *The Consecrated Life, A Comparative Commentary of the Eastern and Latin Codes* (Ottawa: Faculty of Canon Law, Saint Paul University, 2008), 324.

[4] Jobe Abbass gives an excellent history and understanding of the matter in "The Admission of Eastern Catholics to the Novitiate of Latin Religious Institutes," *Studia Canonica* 36 (2002) 293-318.

point out that you anticipate her admittance to first profession very soon, and that you would like her to make profession with the other novices.

Since your institute is of diocesan right, the diocesan bishop should also write a letter. He should indicate that he understands what happened, and that he supports this petition. After organizing these materials, send them to the Prefect of the Congregation for the Oriental Churches, through the Apostolic Nuncio's office in Washington, DC. When the rescript arrives, it will ask for payment of an administrative tax.

Eileen C. Jaramillo, J.C.L.

CONTRIBUTORS

REV. MSGR. MARK L. BARTCHAK, J.C.D., is Judicial Vicar and Vicar for Canonical Affairs of the Diocese of Erie, Pennsylvania.

REV. ROBERT R. CANNON, J.C.L., is the former Judicial Vicar for the Diocese of Venice, Florida, serving currently as a chaplain in the United States Air Force.

REV. THOMAS E. CRONKLETON, JR., J.C.D., is Judicial Vicar for the Diocese of Cheyenne, Wyoming and Pastor of Holy Trinity Parish in Cheyenne, Wyoming.

REV. BRENDAN DALY, J.C.D., is the Principal, Good Shepherd College, Auckland, New Zealand, and Associate Judicial Vicar of the Regional Tribunal of New Zealand.

WILLIAM L. DANIEL, J.C.L., is Vice-Chancellor and Director of the Tribunal of the Diocese of Winona, Minnesota.

REV. MSGR. FREDERICK C. EASTON, J.C.L., is Judicial Vicar in the Archdiocese of Indianapolis, Indiana.

JAMES-DANIEL FLYNN, J.C.L. is Episcopal Liaison for Canonical Affairs in the Archdiocese of Denver, Colorado.

REV. MARK J. GANTLEY, J.C.L. is Judicial Vicar and Director of Canonical Affairs in the Diocese of Honolulu, Hawaii.

CHAD J. GLENDINNING, J.C.L., is a Defender of the Bond of the Canadian Appeal Tribunal in Ottawa, Ontario, Canada.

REV. PAUL L. GOLDEN, C.M., J.C.D., is Director of Vincentian Canonical Services in Denver, Colorado.

JOHN M. HUELS, J.C.D., is on the Faculty of Canon Law at Saint Paul University in Ottawa, Ontario, Canada.

EILEEN C. JARAMILLO, J.C.L., is a Canonical Consultant and Collegiate Judge in the Diocese of Lansing, Michigan and an Adjunct Faculty Member at Siena Heights University in Adrian, Michigan.

REV. PATRICK R. LAGGES, J.C.D., is the Director of the Hesburgh Sabbatical Program at the Catholic Theological Union and Chaplain at Calvert House at the University of Chicago.

REV. AUGUSTINE MENDONÇA, J.C.D. is Professor Emeritus of the Faculty of Canon Law at Saint Paul University in Ottawa, Ontario, Canada and Pastor of St. Mary's Parish, Carleton Place, Ontario, Canada.

REV. BRUCE MILLER, J.C.L., is Moderator of the Curia and Judicial Vicar for the Diocese of Alexandria, Louisiana.

EDWARD N. PETERS, J.D., J.C.D., holds the Edmund Cardinal Szoka Chair at Sacred Heart Major Seminary in Detroit, Michigan.

LAWRENCE G. PRICE, J.D., J.C.L., is Assistant Professor of Business, and Adjunct Professor of Pastoral Ministries, at St. Mary's University in Winona, Minnesota.

REV. MSGR. JOHN A. RENKEN, J.C.D., is Professor of Canon Law at Saint Paul University in Ottawa, Ontario, Canada.

SIOBHAN M. VERBEEK, J.C.L., is Associate Director of the Secretariat of Doctrine, and Co-staff to the Committee on Canonical Affairs and Church Governance, of the United States Conference of Catholic Bishops in Washington, DC.

REV. WILLIAM H. WOESTMAN, O.M.I., J.C.D., is Associate Episcopal Vicar for Canonical Services in the Archdiocese of Chicago, Illinois.